AS SEEING THE INVISIBLE

Choosing rather to share ill-treatment with the people of God
than to enjoy the fleeting pleasures of sin.
He considered abuse suffered for the Christ greater wealth
than the treasures of Egypt, for he looked to the reward.
By faith he left Egypt, not being afraid of the anger of the king;
for he endured as seeing him who is invisible.

HEBREWS 11:25-27

AS SEEING THE INVISIBLE

A STUDY OF THE BOOK OF REVELATION

by D. T. Niles

SCM PRESS LTD
BLOOMSBURY STREET LONDON

FIRST BRITISH EDITION 1962
FIRST CHEAP EDITION 1964

TYPESET IN THE UNITED STATES OF AMERICA
AND PRINTED IN GREAT BRITAIN BY
BILLING AND SONS LIMITED
GUILDFORD AND LONDON

CONTENTS

D. T. NILES: A PERSONAL APPRECIATION
by Henry P. Van Dusen

My first meeting with D. T. Niles was more than twenty years ago. A comparatively young man barely forty, I had been sent to Madras in 1938 to chair the First Section of the World Missionary Conference at Tambaram, a conference notable among other reasons for the unprecedented youth of its leadership. I was informed that the secretary of the Section was to be a Ceylonese ten years my junior; and I was told that he was regarded as one of the most gifted and promising younger Christians of southern Asia. For the better part of three weeks we sat and toiled literally shoulder to shoulder in fashioning the Madras Conference statement on "The Faith by which the Church Lives."

An association thus begun has broadened and deepened across two decades. In 1960, it was my privilege to welcome Dr. D. T. Niles to Union Theological Seminary as Harry Emerson Fosdick Visiting Professor, chosen from among all the Christian scholars of Asia, Africa, and Latin America as the first Younger Churchman to be appointed to that chair whose previous occupants had included Dr. George MacLeod, Principal John Baillie, and Professor Hendrik Kraemer.

The forecast of those early years has been abundantly fulfilled. D. T. Niles soon became the acknowledged spokesman for Christian youth not only of his own land and of Asia but of the whole world. Shortly after the Madras Conference, he left Ceylon to undertake his first ecumenical post as evangelism secretary of the World's Committee of Y.M.C.A.'s. At the Amsterdam Assembly in 1948, he was appointed first chairman of the Youth Department of the World Council of Churches. But his gifts of leadership were not limited to youth. He was chosen to preach the sermon at the service which opened the First Assembly of the World Council at Amsterdam—"a remarkable utterance, incisive, theological, hopeful," the Official Report described it. From 1953 to 1958, he served the World Council as secretary of its Evangelism Department. But his initial loyalty to the church of his motherland was never surrendered. He guided the National Christian Council of Ceylon as its general secretary in the early nineteen-forties. He continued as an active minister of the Methodist church of that country, on temporary leave for successive ecumenical tasks, and has held several local pastorates as well as the principalship of Jaffna Central College. When the churches of Asia began to project a regional ecumenical body of epochal significance, one person was desired as first general secretary of the East Asia Christian Conference, the position he now discharges.

In the meantime, D. T. Niles was sought as a principal speaker at almost every world or national Christian gathering. And his dozen books have made him known to an even wider audience, for they speak with the same disarming directness, the same deceptive simplicity, often frankly in the first person, always unmistakably straight from the core of personal certitude and the heart of personal assurance. Like the mind of their author, they are strikingly free from the involved argumentation, the ponderous effort after impressiveness, which so often characterize Western habits of Christian speech. No man's judgment is infallible; but times beyond numbering I have witnessed this man pierce through a fog of confusion and a maze of subtle rationalization to lay bare the real issue with uncanny accuracy and to set it forth with compelling clarity. Through him, the unique gifts of the oriental perception of Christian truth find superlative expression.

Dr. Niles tells us that Revelation has been his constant companion, his favorite book of Scripture, throughout his ministry. Into this volume he has gathered the fruits of more than two decades of reflection, meditation, study, and composition. The manner of presentation is as original, as unexpected, as suggestive as its matter. For many who, like myself, have always found the Apocalypse forbiddingly obscure, elusive, and uncongenial, it will disclose unsuspected riches. It is certain to lure many to a fresh wrestling with a difficult text which has so manifestly illumined and fortified Dr. Niles. I do not hesitate in venturing the judgment that this is much the best and most important book which D. T. Niles has yet given us. Among its most valued gifts will be the entrance it opens into the inmost soul of one of the rarest as well as one of the most respected molders of the World Christian Movement in our time.

PREFACE

The book of Revelation is a wonderful country both for the tourist and for the pilgrim. It is also an exciting country for the archaeologist. The present study, however, is only a first guide for those who would visit there. Its primary concern is not to open up all the riches of interest that this country affords, nor to provide answers for the many questions which a visitor might ask, but so to help those who come that at least they may be led to love this land and, loving, may be persuaded to spend time therein.

There are many problems which anyone who writes on the book of Revelation must face. First of all, there are the many views as to what kind of book it is. Is it a prediction of future events, is it an exposition of a particular historical situation in allegorical language, is it a collection of apocalyptic oracles? Second, there is the opinion, widely held, that the book in its present form is the work of a redactor; and that he has not only rearranged John's material, often unskillfully, but also introduced new material of his own. There is no discussion of these many questions in this book. A bibliography, however, is given for the guidance of those who desire to pursue a study of them.

Here, on the other hand, the sequence of the book of Revelation as now found, is left practically unaltered and, in order that it may speak for itself, the device has been employed of weaving together text and interpretation into a direct communication such as John himself can be imagined as sending to the churches. Often the book of Revelation is spoiled for the reader by too much marginal comment about passages—their origins, position, allusions, and meaning. Such treatment cuts up the book into discrete episodes obscuring the drive of its argument and spoiling the passion of its narrative.

John is a poet. His images are intended to suggest meaning. A literal interpretation of them, therefore, would be misleading. John's book is also prophecy and apocalypse so that it cannot be used legitimately to provide a sketch of the course of history. It is rather the proclamation of God's will for, and God's judgment on, the immediate situation: the proclamation being made, nevertheless, in terms of the whole gospel and the light it sheds on the whole story of man. John is also a confessor. He has suffered for the faith because he discerned with concrete particularity the eternal issues as they presented themselves to him. His book is aimed at helping others to do the same. It is not the work of a doctrinaire but of one who writes responsibly.

Indeed, the essential message which John is seeking to deliver is such that even major differences of interpretation do not affect it. This is so to such an extent that they who but skim the pages of his book become aware of its dominant theme: its impassioned protest against all earth-bound ultimates and its enthusiastic certainty in the victory of the will and design of God.

> Workman of God! oh, lose not heart,
> But learn what God is like,
> And in the darkest battle-field,
> Thou shalt know where to strike.
>
> Thrice blest is he to whom is given
> The instinct that can tell
> That God is on the field when He
> Is most invisible.
>
> . . . .
>
> For right is right, since God is God,
> And right the day must win;
> To doubt would be disloyalty,
> To falter would be sin.[1]

The eternal world which John uncovers is independent of time. Yet, it is constantly near, always within reach, impinging on human history and breaking through in decisive action as unexpected as the coming of a thief. As Paul expresses it, we are those "upon whom the end of the ages has come."[2] This means that the end of all time is already present as hidden fact, and that again and again there will come that experience of an open vindication of it which is both its guarantee and its foretaste. John speaks triumphantly of such an experience, which he sees awaiting the Church of his own day: its Easter after its passion and crucifixion. He could not have known the form in which his

[1] Frederick William Faber, from "On the Field."
[2] I Cor. 10:11.

anticipation would come true, but come true it did when, within three hundred years of his writing, even the forms of common life of the people came under the controlling influence of the Church.

The book of Revelation is the final summons of the Scriptures to the life of obedience in faith, so that its full impact is felt only as memory provides those quotations from the rest of the Bible which lie behind its own vivid expression of them. In this study, both in the Introduction and in the footnotes, the relation that exists between the book of Revelation and the other books of the Bible is set out. Also, there is at the end of this study a series of theological meditations which follow the divisions of the text and set them in the context of biblical teaching as a whole. It is not only necessary to recognize that the teaching of the book of Revelation is in full accord with that of the rest of Scripture, but it is also essential to meditate on it until God's Word to oneself is born thereby. This is not simply a letter of John to the Christians in Asia; it is a communication from the Lord to the Christians of all lands and every generation.

There is one thing more to say in this Preface. Throughout my ministry the book of Revelation has been for me a constant companion. In fact, I began this study of it some twenty years ago, during the Second World War, as a search for biblical guidance on the many issues that were being discussed within the Church at that time. Now, as I send out this book for publication, it also gives me great satisfaction that it was written in the twenty-fifth year of my ordination. No gratitude is adequate for the privilege of having been a preacher and pastor these many years. Yet this book is an act of thanksgiving. Through it, I seek to commend the gospel in the service of which I have sought and in some measure have been enabled to live.

I have dedicated this book to my wife and sons; to my wife, for the twenty-fifth year of my ordination is also the twenty-fifth anniversary of our marriage—how often we have administered the sacrament of His grace to one another!—and to my sons, both of whom began their theological training in this same year. My wife and I could have asked for no more satisfying evidence of God's gracious way with us than this token by which our sons have been led to choose to become preachers.

God guides His children round many blind corners. He knows the way they must take. It is the Devil who indulges men's desire to see the whole road ahead; he hides only the precipice at the end of the road. The first book of the Bible describes man as "having his eyes opened" when he sinned; the last book of the Bible would help men to see: to see the conflicts and contests of earth from the point of view of heaven, to look beyond these conflicts and contests at the appearance of the invisible. So obedience is made possible in the light of faith, and God becomes man's dwelling place.

But living where the Sun
Doth all things wake, . . .
. . . I consent and run
to ev'ry myre;
And by this world's ill-guiding light,
Erre more than I can do by night.[3]

There is in God, . . .
A deep but dazzling darkness: as men here
Say it is late and dusky, because they
See not all clear.
O for that Night, where I in him
Might live invisible and dim![4]

D. T. NILES

December, 1960

[3] Henry Vaughan, from "The Night."
[4] *Ibid.*, from "Dear Night, This World's Defeat."

INTRODUCTION

Occasion
Authorship
Address
Apocalypse

The book of Revelation is part of Scripture, so that an adequate understanding of it is essential for a right appreciation of the biblical message as a whole. This is all the more true during times such as these when the sin of men and of nations is yielding such rich harvest, and the common man is asking what the meaning of life's tragedy may be. Are men completely at the mercy of their fellows, or does God control the purposes and designs of men? Is a man shut within the consequences of his sinning, or is there with God a love and patience which can break the power of sin: Is history the mere working out of natural laws and forces, or does God's almighty hand shape the form of coming events: Does this world hold its meaning within it, or is there another world in whose light this world must be understood? How does the church discharge its task as "watchman," or are there times when it may renounce responsibility for the ordering of the world? The book of Revelation has light to shed on all these questions. It too belongs to a day when for men the seals of time were breaking, and the world as they knew it was hurrying to a close; when the trumpets of alarm were sounding and the problems of life were summoning men to the "alert"; when across the whole scheme of earthly order the vials of God's judgment were being poured, bringing an era to its consummation.

Occasion

John wrote his book at a time of grave peril for the Church. Persecution had broken out and many had already suffered for the faith. John himself was an exile on Patmos. And, although the name of only one martyr is mentioned—Antipas[1]—many more had been slain for the Word of God and for the testimony which they held. The phrase, "the testimony of Jesus,"[2] seems to have been a technical term used in John's day for that confession of the Church with which the early Christians confronted the world.

What had caused this persecution? The book of Revelation makes the answer plain. Persecution was the result of earthly power defending itself in rebellion against its heavenly King. Christus Imperator,

[1] Rev. 2:13.
[2] Rev. 1:2, 9; 6:9; 12:17, 19:10.

Christus Pantokrator, Christus Victor: the Ruler of the kings and the kingdoms of the earth was exercising His rule, and those who would not submit had to contend. It is because this is so that it behooves the Church to suffer with hope and patience whether the attempt be to destroy it or to domesticate it. Persecution was, and always is, pressure applied to make the Church serve subordinate ends (in the time of John—the unity of the Roman empire and its peoples) or adjust its witness to Christ to the beliefs of those who will not name Him Lord.

At first, the main source of hostility was the Jews, a hostility which was present right up to the time of John, and which even in the year 155 was effective enough to cause the martyrdom of Polycarp in Smyrna. Also, apart from martyrdom, the Christians suffered at the hands of the Jews from periodic outbursts of mob violence which issued in looting[3] and physical cruelty.

This attitude of the Jews toward the Christians was due to two main reasons. The Christians claimed that the "felon" Jesus was the Messiah. This was blasphemy. The Christians also were robbing Judaism of many among the Gentiles who had attached themselves to the Jewish faith. These "god-fearers" as they were called, attracted by the monotheism and the ethic of Judaism but unable to accept its rite of circumcision and its food laws, were becoming Christians in large numbers.

During the early years, however, when the Christians suffered from the hostility of the Jews, the Roman government was, on the whole, tolerant of the Christians. This policy of tolerance is reflected in the narrative of the Acts of the Apostles, and explains also the way in which Paul and Peter write about the Roman state.[4] Although these epistles were written during the time of Nero, they belong to the early period of Nero's reign when wise men like Burrus and Seneca were his chief advisers.

But soon this attitude of tolerance gave place to one of suspicion, a change for which Christianity itself was largely responsible. Its refusal to be one religion among many, and its insistence on its right to evangelize had already roused the enmity of the Jews. From the

[3] Heb. 10:34.
[4] Rom. 13:1-7; I Pet. 2:13-17.

Roman standpoint this enmity between Jew and Christian was serious, for it caused disunion within the empire. Also, the Christians aggravated this disunity by keeping aloof from the social life of their fellow citizens.

They could not do otherwise, for such social life as there was included idolatrous practices in which they could not participate. But the result was that they set themselves apart as a community which was dangerously different. To add to all this, there was a serious misunderstanding of them caused by their being a secret society. No non-Christian was admitted to their worship, and because of the language of their ritual they were accused of eating the flesh and drinking the blood of human sacrifices. They also roused the suspicion of the Roman authorities who disapproved of all secret societies as potential sources of disaffection within the empire.

It was inevitable that the state should seek to check this disruptive consequence of Christianity on the body politic, and it did so in the only way it knew. It enforced common acceptance of the religion of the state, seeking thus to preserve the unity of the empire as well as to deal with the absolutist claims of Christianity. (The Jews were the only people who were exempted from conformity to the state religion. They were only expected to pray for the emperor in their synagogues.)

Roman religion was essentially national. It was not so much concerned with the honor of the gods as with the welfare of the state. It permitted every species of private belief and practice as long as the people evidenced their loyalty to the state by participating in the state religion. As the Roman authorities saw it, no issue of "worship" was involved in this. The Christians, however, saw more deeply into the consequences of accepting the religion of the state. It meant not only accepting the right of the state to claim the absolute obedience of its citizens, it meant also accepting the claim of the state to autonomy. This could not be granted, for the true Lord, both of the individual as well as of the nation, was Jesus Christ. He who was man's Savior from sin was also the Ruler of the kings of the earth.[5]

The development of Roman state religion was a natural and a gradual one. Even while Rome was still a republic, the spirit of the

[5] Rev. 1:5; 17:14; 19:16; cf. Ps. 89:27.

state had been personified as the goddess Roma, and there was a temple for her in Smyrna as early as 195 B.C. Thus it was but a natural step, with the advent of the emperors, to include them also as objects of reverence, since it was they who wielded the power and authority of the state. It was true that Julius Caesar in his pride, Caligula in his madness, and Domitian in his cruel ambition claimed divinity for themselves as individuals: but the issue of state religion always remained one of loyalty to the state as such and of securing the unity of the empire.

This issue of conformity to the state religion, however, was not the cause of the persecutions which the Christians had to suffer under the earlier emperors. At that time neither the state nor the Church had sharpened this issue. All that was present was a growing suspicion of the Christians which afforded a pretext for emperors like Nero to indulge in sporadic outbursts of cruelty against them. But with Domitian, in whose reign the book of Revelation was written, persecution was the result of deliberate decision; it was also empire-wide, extending to and including Asia. The Christian faith endangered the unity of the empire and called into question the position of the emperor; therefore, it had to be suppressed.

The edict that Domitian issued laid down that all his subjects should burn incense to him as "Lord and God" and that those who refused should be punished. Also, it was provided that those who supported the Caesar cult should wear a special mark, with the result that those who did not have the mark were boycotted in the markets and ostracized in social life.[6]

In Asia, this edict of Domitian was enforced by the "Commune." The Commune consisted of the representatives (Asiarchs) of the chief Asian cities.[7] Meetings of such a body took place as early as 95 B.C. during the time of the Pergamenian kings.

When separate cities associated to form a union, the normal practice was for them to sign a treaty involving the common performance of rites by representatives of both sides. These rites might be performed either to the patron gods of the two cities or to some god or gods chosen by common consent. The representatives who formed the

[6] Rev. 13:15-16.
[7] Acts 19:31.

Commune, insofar as they performed these rites, were also the priests of the common worship. When Asia came under Rome, Rome continued the institution of the Commune for the purpose of fostering unity: and soon the Commune did even better than Rome expected when, with the fall of the republic and the founding of the empire, they adopted the worship of Caesar as the common Asian cult.

Amid the misgovernment and rapacity that attended the last years of the republic, Asia suffered terribly. Hence it welcomed the advent of the empire, which inaugurated an era of comparative peace, order, and respect for property. Augustus had been a savior to the Asian peoples and they worshiped him as the "present diety."

Thus the imperial cult and its administration through the Commune were a natural growth in Asia and were supported by common practice and sentiment. As time went on, however, and the pre-imperial miseries were forgotten, the worship of the emperor ceased to satisfy the people, for as religion it had no power to satisfy man's spiritual need; and the practice was adopted of identifying the divine emperor with the local god. This practice had already begun in the time of Domitian.

The result was that in opposing emperor worship, the Christians found themselves in opposition not only to Rome but also to local custom. Pergamum was the seat of the Commune in John's day. "Satan's throne" is what he calls it.

The necessary result of all this pressure upon the Christians was that many found it too great and tended to compromise, while some even sought to falsify the issue. The book of Revelation is as much a warning against these as it is a warning against the claims of Rome. For where there is tribulation without, it is important to deal conclusively with the temptations within. John uses three names to describe this group which was such a source of weakness in the life of the Church. He calls them "Nicolaitans," "Balaamites," and "the followers of Jezebel."[8]

According to Irenaeus, who wrote about the year 185, the Nicolaitans were the followers of Nicolaus, a proselyte of Antioch.[9] They were Gentile Christians who set at nought the instruction of the

[8] Rev. 2:6, 14-15, 20-24.
[9] Acts 6:5.

apostolic Church that they "abstain from meat sacrificed to idols . . . and from fornication."[10]

It was a fact of the social life of the time that all feasts were made in honor of some god and were often held in halls within the temples themselves. A Christian who sought to obey the apostolic injunction not to eat meat sacrificed to idols was, therefore, forced to cut himself adrift from ordinary social life. Many Christians who were business men and who belonged to trade guilds found this a serious problem. So they began to take refuge behind another piece of apostolic advice. Paul had advised that there was no harm in buying from the market meat which had been offered to idols (most meat in the market was of this kind), and it began to be argued that there was no harm, either, in attending a feast even though it was held in honor of some god, and the food served had first been offered to it.[11] As for the question of fornication, it was closely connected with that of attendance at pagan feasts, because such were the associations of the temples in which these feasts were normally held.

The names of Balaam and Jezebel as applied to the Nicolaitans show also that the problem was one of marriage with unbelievers. Balaam led Israel to marry among the women of Moab; while Jezebel, because of her marriage, introduced pagan religious practices into Israel.[12]

What were the grounds on which the Nicolaitans based their practice of compromise? They based it on two grounds: the first they called "the principle of liberty,"[13] and the second "the principle of mystery."[14] They contended that Christ had set men free from the discipline of the law and that therefore men were free from binding norms. They also contended that the spiritual life to which Christians were called should not set them apart from the material life; and that only he knew what true spiritual life was who also had entered into the full mystery of material existence, who knew, as they said, "the deep things of God." On the principle of liberty, attendance at pagan

[10] Acts 15:29; cf. Rev. 2:14.
[11] I Cor. 8:7-13; 10:20-30.
[12] II Pet. 2:15; Num. 25:1; 31:15-16; I Kings 16:31.
[13] II Pet. 2:19.
[14] Rev. 2:24; cf. I Cor. 2:10.

feasts was permitted; on the principle of mystery, fornication was condoned.

It is of course clear that the Nicolaitan principles were brought in to rationalize a course of action that was undertaken on other grounds. Of the three cities where the Nicolaitans were strong—Ephesus, Pergamum, and Thyatira—Ephesus was the center of a national religion, that of Diana; Pergamum was the center of emperor worship; and Thyatira was the center of big business.

The Church was engaged in a life-and-death struggle with the world, the flesh, and the Devil; and there could be no compromise with any one of the three. The Church's public witness to Christ would have no significance if its inner life were already occupied by other gods.

Authorship

For a book written with such authority, there is no indication in the book itself as to who its author was. "I, John"—that is all, and it must mean that the writer was well known and held a position of unquestioned influence in the life of the churches to which he wrote.

During the period when the canon of the New Testament was being formed, the book was attributed to John, the son of Zebedee, one of the twelve. But soon scholars questioned this assumption, not only because of lack of positive evidence, but because of strong dissimilarities in style, language, and patterns of thought between the book of Revelation and the Fourth Gospel. Dionysius of Alexandria who died in A.D. 265, and who was a pupil of Origen, was the first to suggest that the Fourth Gospel and the book of Revelation could not have been by the same person; and since that time biblical scholarship has largely confirmed this opinion. Indeed, there is no way of identifying the author of the book of Revelation. Happily, however, neither the interpretation nor the authority of the book are dependent on solving this problem of authorship. It is simply enough to know that John, the seer, was one of the greatest gifts of God to the Church of his day; and that the Church of all ages has cause to be thankful for the strength of his faith, the certainty of his hope, the clarity of his vision, the glow of his imagination, and the fervor of his writing.

John saw his visions and wrote his book on the island of Patmos.

He was there "on account of the word of God and the testimony of Jesus." During the imperial period, according to Pliny the historian (A.D. 112), banishment to one of the islands off the mainland of Asia was a common form of punishment. Such banishment, in the case of important persons, was often only a form of exile, while in the case of others it was accompanied by a sentence to hard labor. At Patmos, a small, rocky island about fifteen miles from Ephesus, there were stone quarries, and, according to Victorinus (a commentator of the fourth century), John in his banishment was also under sentence to work in these quarries. Breaking stones in the heat of the sun under the eye of overseers, John nevertheless was aware not of his immediate condition but of his right of entry into the presence of God and the hosts of heaven. This right John exercised, and in reading what he has written one can feel his soaring spirit defying both the hardness of his condition and the weariness of his body.

The book has been dated by scholars as in the reign of Domitian because this date seems to fit best the conditions of the world and the Church as they are portrayed in the book. Irenaeus explicitly says, "This vision was beheld, not in some remote time, but almost in our own generation at the end of the reign of Domitian." It was in the last year of his reign (A.D. 95-96) that Domitian issued his decree concerning emperor worship.

However, controversy has always surrounded the book of Revelation with respect to both its authorship and its date; which controversy together with the strangeness of the book itself militated against its acceptance into the canon of Scripture. Indeed, there seems to have been a division of opinion about it from the very beginning; for while the Muratorian Canon (A.D. 170) includes it, and Western fathers used it, in the Eastern Church there was great hesitation about it, the first Eastern commentary on it appearing only in the fifth century. The influence and opinion of Athanasius seems to have been what finally overcame all hesitations, and secured for the book its assured place as part of Holy Scripture.

ADDRESS

The seven churches to which the book of Revelation is addressed were in seven leading cities of Asia, and the order in which the seven churches are mentioned is the order in which they lay on one of the ancient routes of the Imperial Post. Any messenger sent to them would normally visit them in that order.

At the time that John wrote, and for a long time before that, Asia Minor was the chief center of Greek culture. Hellas had declined, and it was Ionia which had preserved the great tradition of Greece. It was the land of Homer. Also, in New Testament times it was the great center of intellectual activity in the Roman empire. Paul during his missionary journeys stayed longest at Ephesus, and tradition associates Ephesus not only with John the Apostle but also with Mary, the mother of the Lord. Asia Minor, at that time, contained the largest proportion of Christians and, when Jerusalem fell, Ephesus became the center of the Christian Church.

In writing to the seven churches, John is writing to the whole Church. Not only does the number "seven" suggest this, but in New Testament thought it was the whole Church which was present in any local church. Each letter is for all.

There are allusions in all the letters to features of the cities in which the churches were. These allusions, which would have been clear to the original readers, enhance and illustrate the messages which the letters convey.

Ephesus: The city of Ephesus lay on the left bank of the river Caÿster. In many inscriptions it is designated as "the first and greatest metropolis of Asia." It was the center of Roman administration.[15] It was also the western terminus of the great system of Roman roads. In it met the great trade route from the Euphrates by way of Colossae and Laodicea, the road from Galatia through Sardis, and the highway that came up from the south from the Maeander valley.

From its devotion to Artemis (Diana), Ephesus[15] appropriated to itself the title "temple warden." But this phrase took on an additional meaning and came most commonly to be applied to a city which was warden of a temple of the imperial cultus. A second-century inscription speaks of Ephesus as being warden of two imperial temples.

[15] Acts 19:38, 35, 19; cf. I Tim. 1:6-7.

Ephesus was also a hotbed of every kind of cult and superstition and, with respect to the church, was a place where Judaizing and Gnostic teachers early showed themselves active.[15]

The church at Ephesus was founded by Paul.

Smyrna: The ancient city of Smyrna was destroyed early in the sixth century and refounded in the third century B.C. During the period between, it was a city that for all intents and purposes was dead.[16] It is, however, the only city of the seven which is still in existence.

From the time of its refounding, it was a prosperous city and a faithful ally of Rome. It was the guardian of three imperial temples. It also had a strong Jewish colony.[16] The reference in the letter to Smyrna to the antagonism of the Jews to the Church and the martyrdom which it foreboded was strangely fulfilled in the death of Polycarp in 155.

The glory of Smyrna was a garland of splendid buildings which encircled the hill Pagos. A well-known reference to these buildings was the saying of Apollonius who advised the citizens to prefer a crown of men to a crown of buildings.[16]

Paul is said to have visited Smyrna on his way to Ephesus. Thus the church there is probably of Paul's founding.

Pergamum: Pergamum was the capital city of the Attalids, the last of which dynasty—Attalus III—bequeathed his kingdom, with the exception of a small part, to the Romans. Under Rome it became the center of the imperial cult, gaining the position of temple warden before any other city in Asia. In it were three imperial temples. It had a temple dedicated to Rome as far back as 29 B.C.

Besides these, on the hill behind the city were many heathen temples and altars, chief of which was the temple of Asclepius whose symbol was the serpent. (John's reference to the throne of Satan has thus a double reference.[17]) Pergamum was the base from which the powerful priesthood devoted to the imperial cult operated.

[16] Rev. 2:8, 9, 11. [17] Rev. 2:13.

Thyatira: Thyatira was a weak frontier city which had to be carefully fortified but which could never be made really strong. In peacetime, however, its position gave it many trading advantages. It was a great merchant center. It also had a flourishing dyeing industry. Lydia, the seller of purple, was from Thyatira.[18]

There were in it many heathen temples but no temple founded in honor of the emperors. This does not, however, mean that there was no emperor worship in Thyatira, for the emperor was worshiped in the ordinary temples as well. Indeed, during the time of Domitian the divinity of the emperor had come to be identified with the local deities.

According to tradition, the Christian church at Thyatira ceased to exist toward the close of the second century.

Sardis: Sardis dominated the rich Hermus valley, and was the capital of the ancient Lydian kingdom. It reached the height of its prosperity under Croesus (*ca.* 560 B.C.). On its conquest by Cyrus it sank into obscurity although it recovered some of its former glory under Rome. But notwithstanding, no city in Asia presented a more deplorable contrast of past splendor and present decline.[19]

Its inhabitants had long been notorious for luxury and licentiousness: and this lack of discipline in living had twice in the past been responsible for the fall of the city. For, although the city was fairly well fortified, there was so little vigilance on the part of its defenders that both Cyrus in 549 B.C. and Antiochus the Great in 218 B.C. captured it by climbing up the hill and stealing unobserved within the fortifications.[19]

In Sardis, too, there was no imperial temple as such, but it was the seat of the infamous worship of Cybele, the mother deity of the Phrygians.

Philadelphia: Philadelphia was founded by Attalus Philadelphus (159-138 B.C.) to be a center of the Greco-Asiatic civilization and a means of spreading the Greek language and manners in the eastern parts of Lydia and in Phrygia. It was a missionary city

[18] Acts 16:14.

[19] Rev. 3:1-2, 3.

from the beginning, the apostle of Hellenism in an oriental land.

When it came under Rome, it soon became a "temple warden," receiving the title under Caracalla. Another new name[20] which it took was that of Neo-Kaisereia—City of the New Caesar. There was in Philadelphia, as in Smyrna, a strong Jewish colony who were a source of trouble to the Christian church up to the time of Ignatius.[20]

During the fourteenth century it stood practically alone against the entire Turkish power as a Christian city in a Turkish land. It suffered often from earthquakes, which feature gives relevance to the promise of stability that it receives.[20]

Laodicea: Laodicea was most favorably situated as regards the imperial road system. It formed the point on the great eastern highway where three roads converged and met. Its situation thus fitted it to become a great commercial and administrative city.

It was an important banking center and very prosperous. When it was overthrown by the great earthquake of A.D. 60-61 it was not obliged to apply for an imperial subsidy as the other cities did. "We need nothing"[21] was what the inhabitants said. It was also a manufacturing city, making clothing and carpets from its native black wool, as well as being the seat of a flourishing medical school.[21]

The church in Laodicea was probably a church of Paul's founding. He sent Epaphras there on his behalf and also wrote them an epistle.[22]

The letters of John are letters to the churches, but the churches exist in, and are part of, a complex life as lived in the cities whose names they bear. Christ's message to them is, therefore, also a message to their world. The Church is for the world, and its Lord is the Lord of the world also.

Apocalypse

The word by which John designates the message which he communicates is the word "apocalypse." It is a revelation, an unveiling,

[20] Rev. 3:12, 9. [21] Rev. 3:17, 18.
[22] Col. 4:13, 16.

an uncovering. Three times in the book the affirmation is made: I am the Lord God, the beginning and the ending, the Alpha and the Omega. In 1:8 this affirmation follows a declaration of God's purpose in history, in 21:6 it follows a description of the redeemed state, and in 22:13 it follows a statement on the process of divine judgment. God is unveiled as the Author and Finisher of the course of human history, the Initiator and Fulfiller of the course of world redemption, the Beginning and the Ending of the course of divine judgment. God's plan in creation will be consummated, Christ's work of salvation will be concluded, the Holy Spirit will effect His work of restoring the *Imago Dei*.

Again and again John makes the claim that he is writing as a prophet,[23] which means that he is proclaiming a direct Word of God and not teaching speculative doctrine. "Thus saith the Lord" is the prophet's authentic posture: and the substantiation of John's claim lies in the fact that the message he delivers has been found to apply to age after age. The particular interpretations given time after time to the visions he conveys may have been arbitrary, but just because it is prophecy that he writes, it illuminates the meaning of any time, and affords guidance for living in every age.

But there is a distinction between prophecy and apocalypse, for whereas prophecy is a thrust of the Word of God into the present, apocalypse is also an unveiling of the meaning of the present in the light of the final end. Christian apocalypse is written from the standpoint of the contemporaneousness of the Church to the Christ who is risen and who will come again.

The central affirmations of the Jewish faith were that "God is one" and that "He is righteous." The Hebrew thinkers never swerved from this faith. They refused to allow any hint of the existence of a contrary power which was a challenge to God's godhead. There was only one God and He was righteous. This meant that they had to find an explanation for evil within the strict formula of monotheism, and they did it by the affirmation that the only way of understanding the real meaning of the present was to understand it from the standpoint of the future. When God had finished His work, His justice and purpose would then be seen. This end-event when God shall

[23] Rev. 1:3; 10:7, 11; 19:10; 22:6, 9.

finish His work, the Christian faith proclaims, has already begun. In Jesus, it has happened; and the future will be but the uncovering in glory of something that is already true now as fulfillment and promise in spite of our tears.

Christian apocalypse has also one other concern, and that is to affirm the conclusion of the Church's task. At the heart of his message John makes this affirmation,[24] but when he speaks of the conclusion of the Church's task he does not mean that all men will repent and turn to God, but that the Church's task will be brought to a close by God Himself. It is true that it is "the beast from the abyss" which destroys the two witnesses, but the key of that abyss is with God,[25] and only as God brings to its fulfillment His redeeming work, will He allow evil to enact its last Calvary.

Apocalyptic literature had its greatest vogue between the years 200 B.C. and A.D. 150, at a time when the lives of men were lived in the midst of religious persecution, national suffering, and threatened disaster. This period begins with the excesses of Antiochus Epiphanes, runs through the Maccabean revolt against him, includes the destruction of Jerusalem by Titus, and goes on until the Jewish revolt against Rome under Bar-Cocheba. About thirty apocalypses belonging to this period are known, of which the most important are the book of Daniel, the fourth book of Esdras, the book of Enoch, and the book of Revelation, not to mention apocalyptic material found in other books.[26]

It is this knowledge that the book of Revelation belongs to a specific type of literature which has made it possible to interpret it with relative confidence, for all literature of this type has certain common features.

1. The Message Is Signified

The terms used in apocalyptic writing are symbols. This is partly for the purpose of ensuring secrecy, for an apocalypse is marching orders issued in code; but it is also partly for the purpose of awakening emotional response to the message that is declared. John employs

[24] Rev. 11:7 ff.
[25] Rev. 20:1.
[26] Cf. Isa. 24:1–27:13; Ezek. 38:1–39:29; Mark 13:1-37.

a double device for achieving this result. In the first place, he uses archetypal images which have a naturally strong emotional content: dragon, beast, abyss, throne, feast, horse, key, war, warrior, crown, blood, pit; and in the second place, he assaults the imagination with a tremendous array of color, sound, and form.

Color is added to color: a red horse, a red dragon, a scarlet beast, a woman in purple; white robes, a white throne, a white horse, a white stone, a white cloud; golden harps, golden crowns, a golden cup, golden censers, a golden girdle.

Sound echoes upon sound: thunders, trumpets, the sound of many waters, a lion's roar, harps, hail, a multitude in song, an earthquake, a voice from the altar; the shout "Hallelujah," the cry "Fallen is Babylon," the call "Come," the announcement "It is done," the wail "Woe."

Pictures crowd upon one another: robes dipped in blood, blood up to the bridles, drunk with the blood of the saints; fire from heaven, fire upon the altar, eyes and lamps of fire, lightning in the sky; the fallen star, the hurled millstone, an angel in midheaven, a beast upon the shore.

But, as John makes plain, this exuberance of symbolism offers no license for arbitrary allegorizing. His symbols, to use his own word, are intended to "signify": that is, they should not so much be interpreted as be allowed to awaken the imagination. They are neither representative nor allegorical; but are, as it were, habitations in which the thoughts expressed dwell, and the atmosphere of the habitations is indicative of the nature of their occupants. The apocalyptic sculptor is not so much concerned with portraying his "sitter" as with creating an image in which the sitter's spirit can dwell. The reader is invited to visit these images and to hold converse with those who dwell there. He cannot be a mere spectator, he must participate in the total activity. The drama is the drama of man, and the reader too is included.

Along with this type of signification, however, there is also John's use of traditional symbolism such as eyes for vision, horn for power, white for purity, et cetera. There is, too, the use of numbers with given meanings. This numerology, largely rooted in Jewish story and history, is fairly simple and can be simply set out:

Two: the symbol for "adequate witness"—11:3; cf. Deut. 19:15.

Three: the symbol for "completeness"—1:4-5; 16:19; cf. I John 5:8. (*One-third* is the symbol of incompleteness—8:7; 9:15; 12:4.)

Four: the symbol for "anything that concerns the earth," the earth being thought of as a square with four corners—20:8; 4:6; 7:1; 9:14; cf. Matt. 24:31. (In 14:20, the number "sixteen hundred" is the square of four multiplied by the square of ten. But whereas, as here, the multiplier is one hundred when it concerns the earth, the multiplier is one thousand when it concerns heaven—7:4; 21:16.)

Five: the symbol for "smallness"—9:5; cf. Isa. 30:17.

Six: the symbol for "sin," six being one short of seven, the symbol of "perfection." Also there were six heathen peoples who were deposed by Israel—13:18; cf. Dan. 3:1.

Seven: the symbol for "perfection," perfect unity in diversity; for example, the seven colors of a rainbow or the seven days of a week—1:4; 4:5; 1:12; 5:1; 5:6; 12:3; 13:1; cf. Prov. 9:1. (*Three and one-half* is also the symbol of perfection, but of evil perfection. It is the symbol of the time of the power of evil. The oppression of Antiochus Epiphanes lasted three-and-one-half years—11:2.)

Ten: the symbol for "fullness" or "completeness" achieved in aggregation, and not integration as was the case with seven—17:12; cf. Gen. 24:55. It thus becomes also a symbol for "limitation." To come up to ten is to reach the limit—2:10; cf. Dan 1:12. (*One thousand* is the intensification of the meaning of ten, while *seven thousand* (11:13) is the intensification of the meaning of ten along with the meaning of seven.)

Twelve: the symbol for the "Church," there being twelve apostles and twelve patriarchs; note the repetition of twelve in 21:9-27. (*Twenty-four* is twice twelve, symbolizing the continuous Church of God through Old Testament and New Testament times—4:4. *One hundred forty-four thousand* is the intensification both of twelve and of ten—7:4; 14:1; etc.)

Ten thousand times ten thousand: the symbol for "innumerable," for the highest number that can be represented by Greek notation is 99,999,999—5:11; 7:9.

Symbolism according to the principles of numerology, however, is not the only use of numbers which John makes. In 13:18, he uses the number 666, or (according to some ancient manuscripts) 616. Here, the principle of interpretation is, as John says, that of "counting." It was a common practice in John's time to add the numerical value of the several letters of a name and to use the total as a symbol of the name. This type of calculation was known as gematria.

It would be as well to deal straightway with the interpretation of this number since it has afforded commentators across the years one of the most alluring of false trails. The number 666 has been in turn the number of Mohammed, of the Pope, of Napoleon, and of Hitler. Who was 666? John says that it is the number of the beast. He also says that it is the number of a man. Seven is the symbol of perfection and six the symbol of sin. The beast is sin personified. He is 666.

Who, on the other hand, is the man to whom this number refers? Both numbers 666 and 616 fit the name Nero-Caesar written in Hebrew letters—the name yielding 666 when it is written Neron (the Greek pronunciation) and 616 when it is written Nero (the Latin pronunciation).

It is likely that the number 616 is the more authentic and that it was changed to 666 to achieve the symmetry of the number 6.[27]

2. The Message Is Allusive

The language of apocalyptic writing depends for its effectiveness and power not only on its use of pictures and symbols, but also on the fact that these pictures and symbols are those embedded in current literature.

In the book of Revelation, the literature within which its symbols and pictures are embedded is that of the Old Testament. The books of the Old Testament were the Scriptures of the first Christian community. Its faith and proclamation were "according to the Scriptures." Therefore, it is of immense significance that the last book of the Bible should be one in which the message of the Scriptures comes to a glowing restatement, in which allusion is heaped upon allusion, vision is fused with vision, and echo is followed by echo, until there is a procession of ideas, figures, and events which assault the imagi-

[27] See Adolf Deissmann, *Light from the Ancient East* (rev. ed., New York: Harper & Brothers, 1927), pp 276-278, for discussion of gematria.

nation, awaken memory, and captivate the soul.

A selective reference to those passages in the Old Testament Scriptures to which allusion is made in the book of Revelation will be of significance. Within the four hundred and four verses of the book there are five hundred and eighteen quotations from the Old Testament, apart from countless suggestions of it:

The Opening Vision (1:12-18): *Exod. 25:31 f.; Zech. 4:2; Dan. 7:9, 13; 10:6; Ezek. 1:5 f.; 43:2; cf. Matt. 5:14; 17:2.*

The Throne in Heaven (4:1–5:14): *Isa. 6; Ezek. 1:27-28; 10:2, 20; Dan. 7:9-10; Zech. 4:10; cf. Matt. 5:34.*

The Four Horsemen (6:1-8): *Zech. 1:8; 6: 1:8; Ezek. 14:21; Jer. 15:2-3; cf. Matt. 24: 6-7; Luke 21:10-11.*

The Great Earthquake (6:12-17): *Joel 2:30-31; Isa. 2:19; 34:4; Hos. 10:8; Ezek. 32:7; cf. Matt. 24:29 f.; Luke 23: 30.*

The Sealing of God's People (7:1-8): *Ezek. 9:4.*

The Vision of the Redeemed (7:9-17): *Zech. 3:4; Isa. 1:18; 49:10; cf. John 12:13.*

The Four Trumpets (8:7-12): *Joel 2:1; Exod. 9:24; 7:17-21; 10:21-23.*

The Three Woes (8:13–9:21): *Isa. 14: 12, 31; Joel 2: 1-11; Isa. 5: 26-30; cf. Luke 8:31; 10:18-19.*

The Little Book (10:1-11): *Ezek. 2: 8–3:3; Jer. 15:16.*

The Temple Measured (11:1-2): *Zech. 2:1-5; Ezek. 40:5 f.; cf. Luke 21:24.*

The Two Witnesses (11:3-13): *Zech. 4:11; Mal. 4:5; Ezek. 37:10; cf. Mark 9:13.*

The Dragon and the Beasts (12:1–13:18): *Dan 7:1–12:13; cf. I Pet. 5:8.*

The War in Heaven (12: 7-9): *Isa. 14:12; Secrets of Enoch 29:4-5; cf. Luke 10:18; John 12:31.*

The Great Harvesting (14: 14-20): *Joel 3:13; Isa. 63:1-6; cf. Matt. 13:39-42.*

Nero Redivivus (17:8-18): *Sib. Or., Bk. IV, line 119 f.; Bk. V, line 336 f.*

The Fall of Babylon (18:1-3): *Isa. 21:9; Jer. 51:7, 8, 13; Nah. 3:4.*

The Dirge over Babylon (18:4-24): *Ezek. 26:1–28:26; Isa. 13; 14; 34; Jer. 50; 51.*

The Marriage of the Lamb (19:5-9): *Hos. 2:19; Isa. 54:1-8; cf. Luke 14:12-24.*

The Divine Warrior (19:11-16): *Isa. 63:1-6; 11:4; Ps. 2:9.*

The Millennial Reign (20:4-6): *Secrets of Enoch 32:2–33:2; cf. Matt. 19:28; Luke 22:30.*

Gog and Magog (20:7-10): *Ezek. 38:1–39:29.* (*The idea of the dragon's release after a period of imprisonment is common to Jewish, Persian, and Orphic eschatology.*)

The Last Judgment (20:11-15): *Dan. 7:9-10; 12:1-2; cf. Matt. 25:31-46; 22:11-14.*

The New Jerusalem (21:1–22:5): *Isa. 65: 17; 64:4; 54:11-12; 61:10–62:5; Ezek. 40:1–48:35; Zech. 14:8, 11; Exod. 28:17; cf. Heb. 12:22.*

3. *The Message Is Urgent*

The Christian community is addressed by Peter in his epistle as those "who by God's power are guarded through faith for a salvation ready to be revealed in the last time."[28] The picture here is that of a besieged city refusing to surrender because, while it has been reduced to dire straits, it yet knows that succor is on the way and will arrive before it is too late. That is the kind of hour to which all apocalyptic writing belongs. It brings the urgent message: "Hold on and hold out; the king and his army are coming and soon your victory will be won." The agent of intervention in apocalypse was the Messiah; in the book of Revelation it is the returning Christ.

But when will He arrive? A quality of apocalypse as well as of prophecy is a foreshortening of vision which sets out as imminent that which is certain. But in John's writing there is even more than this. He was under the compulsion of the events and ideas of his own time which seemed to say. "The end is certainly near." Jerusalem, the city of God, had been destroyed (A.D. 70). Also, Rome had shown signs of inner collapse. The fact that between the death of Nero and the accession of Vespasian (A.D. 68-69) there had been three contenders for the throne showed how easily the empire could fall apart. And then there was the widely held belief that Nero himself would return from the underworld as the instrument of divine

[28] I Pet. 1:5.

judgment against Rome (it was even thought at first that Nero was not dead but had fled to Parthia on the eastern frontier of the empire, from whence he would come at the head of a Parthian army) to be himself ultimately destroyed in the final conflict between good and evil.[29] All these seemed to say to John: "Soon it will be the end."

But whatever be the emphasis of John about the time of the end, the way in which his message is set out underlines the essential characteristics of the total biblical message concerning the end, and the coming of the Christ. He is coming and will come. Indeed, it is in this fusion of the continuous present with the certain future that the distinctiveness of biblical eschatology lies.

a. Christ comes in every judgment of God, which means that His coming is dependent on the ripeness of a situation for judgment (2:16). This experience can be both individual and social. It can mean not only the day of reckoning for the individual soul, but also "the sifting of the nations in the sieve of vanity" (Isa. 30:28).

b. Christ comes in mercy through acts of discipline and of chastisement (6:16-17). In this sense, His coming will be like a flash of lightning by which men will see that He is with them and has been with them always. So will they see themselves as they really are. The word "parousia," which Paul uses of the coming of Christ, has this meaning: it is the revealing of a presence always and already there.

c. Christ comes to harvest an age (14:17-20). This is the true meaning of such verses as Matthew 13:39, 49. There is no reference here to "the end of the world." In this sense His coming is periodic, and constitutes in history a series of crises. The word "parousia" carried this meaning also, for it was often used in reference to the periodic visits of the emperor to his different colonies.

d. Christ comes through the actualization of His presence and power in the Church (21:2). This coming is a constant and continual process (Matt. 28:20); a process, however, the fact of which the world recognizes only periodically (20:4; 11:11; 8:1-5).

e. But while in these senses there are many days of the Son of Man (Luke 17:22) there is also a final day, when *He shall come in glory to judge the quick and the dead and to usher in the Kingdom of the Father in its finality and fullness* (21:3-5). This day and this

[29] Rev. 13:3; 17:10-12, 16; 19:19.

hour no man knows, not even the Son, but the Father only (Mark 13:32; I Cor. 15:24).

Within this full-orbed teaching of the Bible concerning the returning Christ lies the significance and character of John's message that the Christ is coming soon. His imminence is in the certainty of His coming as well as in the uncertainty of when it will be. It is in the experience of His continued presence as well as in the experience of being at the mercy of the powers of evil which deny that presence. "I come quickly" means both that it will be soon and that it will be sudden. It also means that it is near because it has already arrived.

O Lily of the King! I speak a heavy thing,
  O Patience, most sorrowful of daughters!
Lo, the hour is at hand for the troubling of the land,
  And red shall be the breaking of the waters.

Sit fast upon thy stalk, when the blast shall with thee talk,
  With the mercies of the king for thine awning;
And the just understand that thine hour is at hand,
  Thine hour at hand with power in the dawning.
When the nations lie in blood, and their kings a broken brood,
  Look up, O most sorrowful of daughters!
Lift up thine head and hark what sounds are in the dark,
  For his feet are coming to thee on the waters.[30]

[30] Francis Thompson, from "Lillium Regis."

THE DRAMA

Preliminary: Title, Address, Greeting, Preface, Contents

The Lord and His Church: The Unveiling of God's Person

The Lord and His World: The Unveiling of God's Purpose

The Lord of All Rule: The Unveiling of God's Power

Seven Last Words

To the Reader

The italicized headings appearing at the top of each page in this section indicate major divisions within the book of Revelation. These same divisions are covered elsewhere in *As Seeing the Invisible*. The Subject Index (p. 190) lists all such headings, enabling the reader to locate related material quickly.

A REVELATION

BY

JESUS CHRIST

granted to Him by God, that he might make it known to His servants concerning the things which must happen, and which will happen quickly,

As signified to His servant JOHN (to whom He sent His angel).

This, which is a faithful account of what I saw, is not so much a disclosure of future events as a revelation of their inner meaning. It is God's WORD—a declaration of God's mind as He wills and works in His universe, and the truth as Jesus witnessed it unto me.

Address

This message which I send to you is PROPHECY. It is an announcement concerning God.

Listen to it, therefore, and lay to heart what I have written therein.

It is sent to you to be read aloud at your services.

Blessed is he who will read it aloud, and blessed are you who will listen.

God's hour is near.

Greeting

John, to the Seven Churches in the province of Asia:
Grace to you and Peace

from the Eternal God, who is and was and is to come; and from His Spirit, who is before the eternal throne in the plenitude of His being and the richness of His operation in the world;

and from Jesus Christ, who is God's faithful Witness, the first of the dead to be born to life, the Ruler of the kings of the earth.

To Him who loves us and has freed us from our sins by His blood and has made us a kingdom, priests to His God and Father, to Him be glory and dominion forever and ever. Amen.

Preface

GOD IS GOD FOREVER. Evil fights against the good, darkness struggles against the light, the rule of the powers of the earth contests the rule of God; but God remains in the midst of conflict the Almighty One, the Lord of hosts in victorious battle against wrong. He is the Alpha and the Omega, who is and was and is to come, the Almighty. From the beginning until the ending He is God.

My brethren, as we face our own trials, let us remember this. For ours is no new struggle but another phase in the age-long war between God and the Devil; and we fight, not without assurance, for the Lord of hosts is with us. But let us remember, also, that God can avail us nothing if we ourselves do not remain true to Him.

It was our Master's word to His disciples that in the world they would have tribulation but that in patience they would win their souls. It was the Father's good pleasure, the Master said, to give them the Kingdom. Our Lord thus sought to prepare His Church for that which has been its experience from the beginning, and which is our experience now.

We have suffered for long from calumny, social ostracism, material loss, and the general hostility of the authorities. Many of our leaders have been banished, and some like Antipas have even been put to death. Nevertheless, not yet as a Church have we in our time been called to suffer martyrdom.

That call, however, will soon come; in fact we see it coming—persecution universal, systematic, and relentless—and how shall we meet it if even now we falter and fail? Many have already denied the faith, more have lost their fervor; while false teachers seek to lead the Church into ways of compromise. Ours is no passing circumstance in which we can compromise as a temporary accommodation. It is a fight to the death between eternal enemies, and we dare not bend or break.

I have suffered with you. You know me as an exile on Patmos, working as a convict in its quarries, because I would not compromise the Word of God or deny the truth to which Jesus bore witness. I write to you, therefore, as one having the right to do so. I would have you ready for the struggle. Be repentant and faithful, alive to the nature of your high calling, and conscious of the true significance of events.

We are the bride of Christ and, though called to suffer, yet it is to our marriage that we are bidden and for which we make ready. The world passes away, but our Bridegroom comes.

Behold, He is coming with the clouds,
and every eye will see Him,
every one who pierced Him;
and all tribes of the earth will wail on account of Him.
Even so, Amen.

JOHN, your brother and comrade
both in oppression and in dominion,
by the patience which is in Jesus.

CONTENTS

It was the Lord's day, the day of our Emperor, Christ, and out there on Patmos, I remembered how that at that time you would be gathered together in worship. As I thought of you and sought to worship along with you in the Spirit, I fell into a trance, and I heard behind me a voice like the blast of a trumpet, loud and clear, saying:

Write in a book and send to the seven churches: to Ephesus, and Smyrna, and Pergamum, and Thyatira, and Sardis, and Philadelphia, and Laodicea.

1. *The things you have seen* (the vision and its significance, 1:12-20);
2. *The things which are* (the condition of the Church and the situation in which she is, 2:1–3:22);
3. *The things to be hereafter* (the future and what will determine it 4:1–22:21).

Then I turned to see who it was that spoke, bidding me address the Church, and lo, it was the Lord of the Church Himself, even her Bridegroom.

THE UNVEILING OF GOD'S PERSON

What was He like? And in what manner did I see Him? I saw Him in the midst of His Church.

The Bridegroom must win His bride. She has to be rescued both from herself and from her enemies. He must come to her, therefore, with judgment and promise. Indeed, that is why all judgment begins in the house of God.[1]

The Opening Vision *1:12-18*

I saw seven golden lampstands, representing your seven churches, and through you representing the whole Church of God. And, in the midst of these lampstands, stood the Lord of the Church tending the lamps.[2] The reality of the Church is the reality of His presence within it.

But, not only did it seem to me that He was in the midst of His Church, it also seemed that the Church was in His hand. He held seven stars in His right hand, each star the symbol of one of you as you actually were. And the Lord who tended the lamps also judged the stars. He was the Eternal One.

> Ephesus! It was you that I remembered when I saw the Bridegroom thus, for you too are in a situation in which you have to discern between the actual and the eternal.

I heard Him speak. His voice was like the sound of many waters.[3] And, at His bidding, the seven spirits, which is His Spirit in its fullness, energized the dead, and dry bones came to life.[4] He was the Life-giving One.

> Sardis! I thought of you when I saw the Bridegroom thus, for you are in need of life. Your life at present is largely pretense.

Who was He, this Bridegroom of the Church, whom I saw? He was Jesus, the Man of history and the Messiah of prophecy, the Son of Man. His eyes flashed like fire, fierce to see; and His feet glowed

[1] I Pet. 4:17.
[2] Zech. 4:2.
[3] Ezek. 3:12.
[4] Ezek. 37:6.

like burnished bronze, strong to trample and subdue.[5] He was the Appointed One.

> Thyatira! I remembered you when I saw the Bridegroom thus, for He comes to search out sin and destroy it. There are those among you whose sin has not been disclosed.

He was attired as a judge. He wore the long robe reaching down to His feet, with the belt of gold across His breast. Also He looked old, for God's judging truth is old. It is from the beginning, written into the very constitution of God's creation. But, old though He was, with head and hair as white as snow-white wool, His countenance was as bright as the unclouded sun shining in its might.[6] He was the Constant One.

> Laodicea! How relevant for you this truth about the Bridegroom seemed to me to be. For you need to learn constancy from Him who is always Amen to God's love.

There also issued from His mouth a sharp two-edged sword, the decisive Word of God which makes war on every lie.[7] He was the Royal One.

> Pergamum! This truth about the Bridegroom is something with which you must reckon. For in your city is the seat of the worship of the emperor. Beware lest you live a lie.

I fell at His feet like a dead man when I saw this vision of Him, but he laid His hand on me and spoke to me. "Fear not," He said, "I am the first and the last, and the Living One; I died, and behold I am alive for evermore."[8]

> Smyrna! I wished that you too heard those words. For you too have been faithful unto death. Like your Bridegroom, the Living One, you too shall live though now you die.

He also said to me, "I have the keys of Death and of Hades." For, even as once God set David as ruler over the house of Israel, God has set Jesus now in ultimate authority over the household of faith. He judges the dead, He resurrects unto life, and from His word there

[5] Dan. 10:6.
[6] Dan. 7:13.
[7] Heb. 4:12.
[8] Matt. 17:6.

is no appeal. He is the True and Holy One. He opens and no one shall shut, He shuts and no one opens.[9]

Philadelphia! Remember these things about the Bridegroom and take courage unto yourself to stand more firmly in your fidelity to your appointment in the household of faith.

Lo, I write to you all in the name of your Lord and mine, the Lord of His Church walking in the midst of the lamps—the guarantor of the Church's calling; and holding the seven stars in His right hand—the guarantee of that calling's fulfillment.

The Letters to the Churches 2:1–3:22

So in obedience to His command did I write in a book, to be sent to you, all that I saw; when the Bridegroom said to me, "Write also seven letters to the seven churches and send them along with your book. For the things which you have seen and about which you have written concern the conflict between the faithful and the ungodly, whereas to the churches must be conveyed first the message that they cannot share in God's triumphant purpose which your book portrays if they do not repent and, by fidelity and soundness of faith, they do not live worthily of their calling. I know the spirit which is peculiar to each church, I know their angels; these angels correspond to the stars in My right hand, to each angel I must speak."

I. Thus Saith the Eternal One to the Church at Ephesus:

I KNOW YOUR DOINGS. I know your hard work and your patient endurance. You have borne up for My sake and have not wearied.[10] I know also that you cannot bear wicked men, and that you have tested those who style themselves apostles—no apostles they!—and have found them out to be liars.

You have done especially well in the way in which you have withstood the practice of the Nicolaitans.[11] You hate it, and I hate it too. In the name of a mistaken nationalism, and under the cover of a false view of freedom, they seek to tempt you, and other Gentile converts like you, to transgress the injunction that you abstain from fornication and from food sacrificed to idols.[12]

[9] Isa. 22:22.

[10] I Thess. 1:3.

[11] Eph. 5:11.

[12] Acts 15:29.

Indeed, being a church in a city which is along one of the highways of the world, you have been exposed to all kinds of wandering preachers.[13] You have shown discretion, however, in your reception of them.

BUT I HAVE THIS AGAINST YOU, that the very controversies, which various kinds of teaching have aroused in your midst, have also created among you a spirit of censoriousness and division.[14] It is good to contend for the truth; it is evil to lose the spirit of charity and love. And love you have lost. You have given up loving one another as you did at first.

REPENT, THEREFORE, remembering the height from which you have fallen, and act as you did at first. If not, I will come to you and remove your lampstand. A lamp needs no stand when its light has gone out.[15] Neither can a loveless church take advantage of her opportunities.

Your city has had to shift its situation again and again as the sea ate into the coast. Beware lest as a church, too, you are shifted from your present position of influence and leadership. Your city is a city of change; your God is the Eternal One.

CONQUER YOUR CHANGEFUL NATURE in My name who am Eternal, and I will give you to eat from the tree of life, which is within the garden of God. Thus will you inherit eternal life.

What I say unto you, I say unto all:
He that hath an ear, let him hear.

II. Thus Saith the Living One to the Church at Smyrna:

I KNOW YOUR DISTRESS. I know how you are being slandered by those who style themselves Jews. They are no Jews, but a very synagogue of Satan. I know also that you have been despoiled of your possessions by mob violence—both by Jew and by pagan—but remember that you are rich even when you are poor.

Your city was for centuries a destroyed city, and yet it lived and still lives on: so, as a church also, is life yours even while others seek to destroy you.

[13] I John 4:1.
[14] Matt. 24:11-12.
[15] Matt. 5:15.

BUT THE DEVIL IS AGAINST YOU, and because it is the Devil, your peril is great. He will put some of you in prison that you may be tested, and to all of you he will bring suffering.[16] Know, however, that it is only for a limited time that you will have to endure, even though endurance will be tested to the limit.

HOLD FAST, THEREFORE, and be faithful even though you have to die for it, and I will give you the crown of life.[17] So shall your city also receive in you a new crown. It will then wear no longer a mere crown of buildings and towers as it does now, nor even the crown of good citizens which her leaders exhort her to put on, but a crown of those who are children of the Living God.

CONQUER THE TRIALS THAT AWAIT YOU, resist if necessary unto death, and the living God will give you life. Thus will you not be injured by the second death which is the death of the soul.

What I say unto you, I say unto all:
He that hath an ear, let him hear.

3. Thus Saith the Royal One to the Church at Pergamum:

I KNOW WHERE YOU DWELL. You dwell where Satan sits enthroned. The throne of God is God's mountain of Zion; but lo, the hill behind your city is covered with heathen temples and altars; while the city itself is the center of the imperial cult. Nevertheless you have adhered to My name. You did not renounce your faith in Me even during the days when My witness, My faithful Antipas, was martyred in your midst.

BUT I HAVE THIS AGAINST YOU, that even as Balaam taught Balak to set a pitfall before the children of Israel to eat things sacrificed to idols and to commit fornication, even so have the Nicolaitans set a pitfall before you, a snare into which some of you have fallen.

REPENT, THEREFORE, and repent now. If not, I shall come quickly to make war with the sword of My mouth, and the Word of God shall slay the adherents of Nicolaus. I am the Royal One, I execute judgment.

CONQUER THE TEMPTATIONS THAT BESET YOU and remember that it is not the Roman emperor who is King. I am King. I will give you

[16] Luke 21:12.
[17] Jas. 1:12.

audience into My presence, protection in danger, and sustenance for life. The white stone which I shall give you will be your pass of admission,[18] the strength of your new name—My name—will be your protection, and the hidden manna which will be revealed when the Messiah comes will be your food.[19]

What I say unto you, I say unto all:
He that hath an ear, let him hear.

4. Thus Saith the Appointed One to the Church at Thyatira:

I KNOW YOUR DOINGS. I know your love and loyalty, your service and patient endurance. I know also that you are doing more than you did at first.

Nevertheless, there is still more that you must do if you would really be strong. Your weakness is like the weakness of your city—built on the frontier, enjoying prosperity in times of peace, and yet, in times of war, impossibly situated to be defended adequately. Beware lest in the church, too, your prosperity is the cause of your weakness.

Most of you are craftsmen and traders, fellow citizens with others in a commercial city. Your income will be enhanced and your position made secure if you join the trade guilds.

But the social life of each guild is centered in banquets under the patronage of some god.

Can you join? Many of you ask, "Why not?" and justify yourselves by saying that the gods are nothing and do not exist.[20] Is that your real reason, or is it only an excuse for doing something that will benefit you? You must guard your faith.

BUT I HAVE THIS AGAINST YOU, that you have yielded so far to temptation as to tolerate within your life, as a church, those who teach the way of compromise. Why do you not set yourselves against that Jezebel of a woman who styles herself a prophetess and seduces

[18] The allusion here is probably to a custom in those days of sending a white tablet as an invitation to a banquet, with the host's pet name for the guest engraved upon it.

[19] II Baruch 29:8.

[20] I Cor. 8:4.

My servants by teaching them to give way to fornication and to eat food which has been sacrificed to idols?

I have given her time to repent, but she refuses to repent. Lo, I will lay her on a sickbed and bring those who flirt with her teaching into more distress; while as for her children, those who accept her, they shall surely die. So will all the churches know that I am the searcher of the inmost heart, and that I requite each according to his works.

HOLD FAST, THEREFORE, to what you have been commanded till such time as I come. I impose no fresh burden on you, who have remained faithful, who have refused to learn "the deep things," as they call them.[21] Freedom to explore the depths of Satan cannot be Christian freedom.

And what mystery of God is there in a teaching that leads to immorality? Am I not the only decisive revelation of God?[22]

CONQUER THE LURE OF YOUR OWN INTERESTS, do My works unto the end, and I will appoint you with authority over the nations even as I myself have been appointed by My Father.[23] You who are weak will then be strong, strong to destroy the nations as with an iron rod,[24] strong to shatter them as a potter shatters his shards, strong to make ready for the day of the Lord. On that day you will receive the Morning Star, you will receive Me.

What I say unto you, I say unto all:
He that hath an ear, let him hear.

5. Thus Saith the Life-giving One to the Church at Sardis:

I KNOW YOUR DOINGS. But though the works you have wrought give you a semblance of life, in reality you are dead.[25] It is so with your city, too, for while it is full of things that suggest prosperity these are but remains of a splendor that is past. And they too are rapidly declining.

Wake up, rally what is still left to you even though it be at the point of death: and you may still live. If not, your very lack of watchfulness will be your complete undoing. Remember it was thus

[21] I Cor. 2:10.
[22] Matt. 24:24.
[23] Cf. Acts 7:35.
[24] Jer. 51:20.
[25] Cf. II Cor. 6:9.

that as a city you lost your freedom twice over, having been stormed by night by the enemy when your watchmen were asleep.[26] You have "works," defences, to make watchfulness useful.

BUT I HAVE THIS AGAINST YOU, that none of your works are complete or adequate. They are all wanting in the eyes of God. Others have been corrupted by danger or error; you have been corrupted by ease.

REPENT, THEREFORE, continually laying to heart and being mindful of all the lessons you have learned. If you will not wake up, I shall come like a thief at an hour which you do not know.

There are, however, a few persons among you at Sardis who have not soiled their raiment. They have kept themselves unspotted from the world. In the world to come, therefore, they shall walk with Me, the Life-giving One, clad in white garments.[27]

CONQUER YOUR LUXURIOUS INDOLENCE, all of you, and I will give you also life—white raiment in token of victory, your name in the book of Life in token of full citizenship in the Kingdom, and recognition of you before God the Father and before His angels.[28]

What I say unto you, I say unto all:
He that hath an ear, let him hear.

6. Thus Saith the True and Holy One to the Church at Philadelphia:

I KNOW YOUR DOINGS, for though you are small in number and are of little strength, you have kept the word which I gave you and have not renounced My name. Lo, I have set a door open before you which no one can shut.[29] To you is the opportunity and privilege of spreading My Kingdom. Indeed, the missionary task is native to your city, for was it not founded and situated as it is for the purpose of propagating Greek culture!

BUT THE JEWS ARE AGAINST YOU—they who belong to the synagogue of Satan, for though they style themselves Jews, they are no

[26] Matt. 24:42.
[27] Those accepted for admission to the Roman senate, or for initiation into one of the mystery cults, or for Christian baptism were accustomed to wear white robes.
[28] Luke 12:8.
[29] I Cor. 16:9; Isa. 26:2.

Jews, but liars. I will make them come and do homage before your feet as they expect the Gentiles to do before them. Thus will they learn that I did love you.

You have not only accepted My patient endurance as having been accomplished for you; but you have also sought to live worthily of it. Hence I will keep you safe, lest you fall, through the hour of trial which is coming upon the whole world to test the dwellers therein.

HOLD FAST, THEREFORE, to what you have, so that your crown of victory be not taken away from you. I, the True and Holy One, am coming very soon.

CONQUER YOUR OPPORTUNITIES and you too shall live the life of them that are true.[30] For to you will be given the stability that comes from fellowship with God and constancy in His service; a share in carrying out God's purposes; the privilege of citizenship in the city of the great King, and full participation in the blessings of the new age.

What I say unto you, I say unto all:
He that hath an ear, let him hear.

7. Thus Saith the Constant One to the Church at Laodicea:

I KNOW YOUR DOINGS. You are neither cold nor hot. I would you were either! But because you are lukewarm I am going to spit you out of My mouth. The spirit of your city has eaten into you, and wealth has corroded enthusiasm. "We need nothing," you boast, "for our city is great.[31] It is a famous banking center, the place of manufacture of cloth and carpets from the glossy black wool of our native sheep, and a seat of medicine for eye disease."

BUT I HAVE THIS AGAINST YOU, that in spite of your boast that you are rich and have got riches by earning it yourself, yet you are miserable creatures, pitiful, poor, blind, and naked. Buy from Me a new and disciplined spirit, for that would be gold refined in the fire.[32] Receive from Me victory in daily living, for that would be rich raiment, and white at that. And let Me give you spiritual vision that you may be free of self-deception. That indeed would be real ointment for the eyes.

[30] Isa. 56:5.
[31] Matt. 22:11-14.
[32] Isa. 55:1.

REPENT, THEREFORE, and be in hot earnest. Remember that I reprove and discipline those for whom I have affection, for love is severe. Behold, I stand at the door and knock, if any man hears My voice and opens the door I will come in and sup with him—his guest; and he with Me—My guest. I am the Constant One, and in my companionship will your fervor find constancy. I am the beginning of the creation of God.[33]

CONQUER YOUR OPULENT COMPLACENCY, and you shall share with Me My place in the coming Kingdom.

What I say unto you, I say unto all:
He that hath an ear, let him hear.

[33] Col. 1:15.

The Unveiling of God's Purpose

The Lord comes as guest but remains as host. "Behold, I stand at the door and knock; if any one hears my voice and opens the door, I will come in to him and eat with him, and he with me."

Human history is the story of His coming. He comes to His Church. He comes to the world. He comes to every individual. Behind the thunder and noise and shout of world happenings, and behind the seeming meaninglessness of individual experiences, it is God who stands knocking, seeking and asking for His own.

Already you have heard the Lord of the Church as He spoke to you. He spoke to you about His judgments as they operate in your midst who are His people. The Lord must begin with His sanctuary.[1] Now, listen to what he will reveal to you about His judgments in the world. Remember, though, that the judgments of God are one indivisible reality, even if at any given period of time they may seem to be particularly on the Church or on the world. And, remember this, too: that the Church of God on earth is an emerging community, that the sons of God are revealed in and through and because of God's judgments as they fall upon the world.[2]

The Throne in Heaven 4:1–5:14

This is how the revelation came to me. I was meditating upon the present and upon the future, when suddenly I saw an open door in heaven. However much the vault of the sky may suggest a world that is closed in, yet those who have eyes to see discern the open door, and know that the God who rules above rules also below.

As I looked at that door I heard the trumpet voice which I had heard before say to me, "Come up hither, and I will show you the things which must necessarily come to pass."[3] No sooner did I hear these words than that, at once, I was in the Spirit and entered through that open door. How different "the things which must come to pass" looked

[1] Ezek. 9:6.
[2] Rom. 8:18-19.
[3] This follows the Revised Version marginal reading which attaches the words translated "hereafter" to verse 2.

as I saw them from the vantage point of heaven. It is not any revelation of the future which we need; our need rather is to see the future from the point of view of God. And that is what God revealed to me, and which now I reveal to you.

Do not therefore misunderstand what I write—thinking that I am predicting future events. I do no such thing. My desire is only to make plain what are the central certainties of the future, whatever may happen. They are God who is the great "I am" and the Lamb, of whose nature is God's authority. This means that there is only one future event which is always happening, happening in and through all other events: the revealing of the sons of God, the unsealing of the scroll of Life.

What did I see in heaven? I saw a throne.[4]

There is a Ruler of the universe, and He rules.

His presence, however, is impossible to describe except as a radiance of jewels. There was the flash of the diamond, brilliant in its purity; there was the light of the ruby, red as blood; while round the throne was a rainbow quietly green as the emerald.[5] God is holy, God is love, and God is peace.

There were also twenty-four other thrones set around the throne, and on these sat the ancients.[6] They were the witnesses of all God's action from the beginning. Yet regal though they were, they fell down and worshiped God. God alone is King, there is no other.

From the throne issued flashes of lightning, peals of thunder, and voices striking terror upon them that would draw near. For God is righteous, and who can stand before Him? Also, in front of the throne seven torches were burning. They illumined the entire universe. They were the symbol of God who sees and knows all.

Moreover, I perceived that God's throne was more than a throne. It was a chariot too. Above the firmament and the crystal sea[7] (which are the waters above the firmament) God rode in His chariot drawn by the four cherubim. These cherubim execute His will unto the four

[4] Isa. 66:1.
[5] Rev. 10:1.
[6] Isa. 24:23; Job 38:7.
[7] I Kings 7:23.

corners of the earth. God's sovereignty is always and everywhere maintained.[8]

The cherubim carried the throne upon their backs, so that while their heads were seen at the corners, their bodies were concealed under the throne. They had each six wings to speed them on their flight. They were also endowed with both vision and insight, having eyes without and within. The first resembled a lion; the second, an ox; the third, a man; and the fourth, an eagle—thus combining among them the majesty and strength, the patience and labor, the wisdom and love, the speed and flight of the persistent working of God.

Also, day and night these cherubim chanted without ceasing, "Holy, holy, holy, is the Lord God, the Almighty, who was and is and is to come." And as they chanted they served Him, rendering by their service, glory, thanksgiving, and honor. And, whenever the cherubim thus glorified Him who was upon the throne, the four-and-twenty ancients too fell down before Him worshiping. They cast their crowns before the throne crying, "Worthy art thou, our Lord and God, to receive glory and honor and power, for thou didst create all things, and by thy will all created things exist." God is Lord, and every rule bows down before Him.

Impossible though it was to see the face of Him who sat upon the throne, I saw nevertheless His right hand. He held in it the scroll of Life.[9] In the scroll were the names of the sons of God, such a multitude that their names filled the scroll and ran over even onto the outside.[10] But the scroll was sealed with seven seals. So that, while it lay on God's open palm ready to be taken and opened, it was not open yet, for no one dared to touch it. An angel cried out with a great voice, "Who is worthy to open the scroll and break its seals?" I too wept, for no one worthy was found.

But even as earth weeps, heaven answers. One of the ancients said to me, "Behold the Lion of Judah's tribe,[11] the Root of David;[12]

[8] Ps. 99:1.
[9] Exod. 32:32; Isa. 4:3; Luke 10:20.
[10] In Jewish thought, "the scroll of Life" was a register of the citizens of God's Kingdom. Also, in Greek and Roman cities a book was maintained containing the names of its citizens. From it the names of those degraded were expunged (Rev. 3:5).
[11] Gen. 49:9. [12] Isa. 11:1.

He has conquered.[11] He is worthy to open the scroll and break its seals. To Him God has given the authority to control the unfolding of time."

But when I looked I saw, in the midst of the throne and of the cherubim and of the ancients, not a lion but a lamb: a little lamb, the lamb of sacrifice with the mark of sacrifice still upon it.[13] However, it was not weak but strong. Love is strong though it suffer. The Lamb had seven horns, the symbol of its strength; and seven eyes, the symbol of its wisdom. And it came forward and took the scroll that lay in the hand of God. Immediately, heaven and earth burst into song. The Lamb was worthy to open the scroll since He Himself was its author. The scroll was the Lamb's scroll of Life.[14]

The song that was raised was a new song.[15] It was outside the set forms of praise. No old form could express the transcendent joy of redemption.[16] The heavenly court were the first to raise the song, while with their praise were mingled the worship of the Church below on earth. The song swelled as the angelic host came in with their sevenfold doxology, until, finally, it rose to a crescendo of exultation as every voice in heaven, and on earth, and under the earth, and upon and in the sea, joined in that praise.

THE HEAVENLY COURT: "Worthy art thou[17] to take the scroll and to open its seals, for thou wast slain and by thy blood didst ransom men for God[18] from every tribe and tongue and people and nation, and hast made them a kingdom and priests to our God, and they shall reign on earth."[19]

THE ANGELIC HOST: "Worthy is the Lamb who was slain, to receive power and wealth and wisdom and might and honor and glory and blessing."

THE WHOLE CREATION: "Blessing and honor, glory and dominion, forever and ever, to Him who sits upon the throne and to the Lamb. Amen."

[13] Isa. 53:7.
[14] Rev. 13:8.
[15] Ps. 96:1.
[16] Cf. Rev. 3:12.
[17] "Worthy art thou"—*Vere dignus*—were the first words of the solemn acclamation with which the emperor's entrance was greeted in triumphal processions.
[18] I Cor. 7:23.
[19] I Pet. 2:9.

The Four Horsemen 6:1-8

All authority belongs to the Lamb and by Him the course of human history is controlled. That is how I saw it. I saw four horsemen exercise authority, but that authority was given to them; besides, it was strictly limited.[20] Indeed, it was clear that while time ran on to its fulfillment with the succession of event on event; it was still the Lamb under whose authority these events happened. The seals of time were broken by Him, and by Him human history was being pressed to its goal.

The scroll of Life, when I saw it, was sealed.[21] The time was not yet ripe for its contents to be disclosed.[22] But, with the breaking of each seal, that time drew nearer. The scroll would be unrolled only as the seventh seal was broken. It is, thus, the breaking up of the world and its order that I am going to describe; but you will see that there is no "breaking up" without its being also a "breaking open." Every event, whether it be the direct consequence of sin, or the result of natural disasters, or even the working of pure evil, also subserves God's purpose, and works for the punishment of evil, the retribution of wrong, and the setting forth of the witness of the children of God.

Let me now describe to you in detail what I saw as I looked down on the earth. I saw the mercy which had ordained that the wages of sin be death. The cherubim called, the cherubim whose task is to execute God's purposes, and at their call four horsemen appeared, each horseman representing one of the results of sin. On earth we see sin in disguise; it is from heaven that we see sin as it truly is in its nakedness and destructive power. And yet, even that power is limited, for the destructiveness of sin is not ordained for pure destruction but for calling men to repentance. It was the Father's purpose that was served by the famine in the far-off land.[23]

The Lamb broke the first seal, and as He broke it, the first cherubim shouted with a voice of thunder, "Come." And there appeared

[20] Rev. 6:8.
[21] Dan. 12:4.
[22] Cf. Rev. 22:10.
[23] Luke 15:14.

a white horse, and on it rode in triumph a man with a bow.[24] He was given a crown, and he went forth conquering and to conquer. What did he symbolize, this figure on a white horse? He symbolized WAR, for war is the first result of sin. The root of sin is selfishness, and war is the clash of one self-interest with another. Individual wars against individual, group wars against group, class wars against class, and nation wars against nation, until, at the last, they beat each other down and all are destroyed.

But why "a white horse"?[25] Does not the white horse belong to the Christ when he comes to execute judgment? Yes, but is it not true that when men wage war they always pretend to be fighting for righteousness? They claim that the horse they ride is white. Also, is it not true that, in spite of human motives, God's judgment does take place through war? When Parthia attacked Rome, was not Rome justly punished?

The Lamb broke the second seal, and as He broke it, the second cherubim shouted, "Come." And out came another horse, bright red. Its rider was permitted to take away the peace of the earth, so that men should slay one another; and he was given a great sword.

What did he symbolize, this figure on a red horse? He symbolized CIVIL STRIFE. War is conflict between opposing interests, but it also always results in conflict among those whose interests should be the same. On the heels of the Roman legions under Titus in Jerusalem, did there not come the Jewish factions tearing one another in the streets?

Civil strife truly takes away "the peace of the earth";[26] it exposes it for what it is. For what is "the peace of the earth,"[27] when there is peace, except the absence of open strife, a calm surface above the currents of ill will!

[24] John finds his symbol for war and judgment in "the rider with a bow." From the time that Vologeses, the Parthian king, had forced a Roman army to capitulate (A.D. 62) the possibility of a Parthian conquest of the West was constantly in the minds of men.

[25] Rev. 19:11.

[26] Matt. 10:34.

[27] This follows the Revised Version marginal translation "peace of the earth" instead of "peace from the earth."

The Lamb broke the third seal, and as He broke it, the third cherubim shouted, "Come." And I saw, and behold a black horse, and its rider had a balance in his hand. And I heard a voice from amidst the cherubim saying, "A denarius for a quart of wheat, a denarius for three quarts of barley; but harm not oil and wine."

What did he symbolize, this figure on a black horse? He symbolized FAMINE. Men cannot take to war and strife and also cultivate the necessities of life. Scarcity of food is inevitable. But, even here, men increase their distress because they will not act with reason. Whereas with his daily wage (a denarius) a man can buy sufficient wheat or barley for his home, he and his family starve because they insist on spending that money on oil and wine. Indeed, you will remember what happened in Asia when the last famine took place. The emperor, Domitian, ordered that half our vineyards should be cut down and the land used for the cultivation of grain, and it was we who protested and had the order withdrawn. We preferred wine to food.

The Lamb broke the fourth seal, and as He broke it, the fourth cherubim shouted, "Come." And there came a pale horse. Its rider's name was Death, and Hades followed him.

What did he symbolize, this figure on a pale horse? He symbolized PESTILENCE. Pestilence is the inevitable result of the slaughter caused by war. There cannot be dead horses and men covering the fields or choking the rivers without giving rise to pestilence. And where pestilence kills, Hades garners. Also, pestilence is as destructive as war; it, too, kills off a fourth part; and in the midst of it beasts of prey roam the earth and possess the land.

The Cry of the Martyrs 6:9-17

The consequences of sin are terrible, and by them God calls men to repent. He also calls them to repent by revealing to them the very instability of earthly life. From time to time, God grants to men to witness the collapse of everything on which they have depended, and so be challenged to turn to Him on whom alone they can safely depend.

This is what I saw next—the collapse of earthly security; and I saw it happen at the cry of the martyrs.[28] A martyr chooses to die rather than be disloyal to God; it is appropriate consequence, therefore, that

[28] Phil. 1:29.

men should learn that life is not worth buying at the price at which they offer it to the martyr.

Four seals were broken, and at the breaking of each of the four, one of the cherubim had called. But, when the fifth seal was broken, it was the martyrs who called. Even as it was at the foot of the altar that the blood of sacrifice was poured, even so from under the altar did the cry rise: "How long, O Master, how long!" Earth had set up an altar of sacrifice in its midst and had slain on it those who bore witness to the Word of God: but earth did not realize that from such an altar would inevitably rise a cry to heaven for vengeance upon it. Remember the words of Jesus, "Fill up the measure of your fathers, that upon you may come all the righteous blood shed on the earth."[29]

But, though the fifth seal was broken and the martyrs' cry was raised, nothing happened. It seemed that yet there was time, time in which martyrdom continued, time in which the cup of martyrdom was filled. However, even while vindication tarried, one knew that it was certain, for already one saw the martyrs clothed in white, the cause for which they died declared victorious.

But soon the sixth seal was broken, and then there was a great earthquake; what better to show the uselessness of gaining the whole world and losing one's own soul than the collapse of the world's very foundations?[30] It is when even the ground that one stands upon is no longer safe that life's ultimate questionings take on heightened meaning.

It was not an ordinary earthquake that I saw, not some simple physical event. It was rather the dissolution of all earthly security. Light became darkness as the sun turned black as sackcloth and the moon became as blood. Man's guide by night disappeared as the stars of the sky dropped down even as a fig tree shaken by a gale sheds her unripe figs. The earth ceased to be home as the sky that covered it was swept aside and rolled up like a scroll. And life itself became uncertain as mountain and island moved out of their places.

In such a time of testing, position was of no avail.[31] There was no safety even for the kings of the earth. The wealth of the rich afforded no security, the power of the mighty afforded no peace. The bondman

[29] Matt. 23:32, 35.
[30] Mark 8:36.
[31] Jer. 9:23.

had no protection in his master, the freedman had no livelihood from his land. All life's bases were shattered, and men hid themselves for fear. They hid in caves and among the rocks and tried to be hidden from God's sight.[32] Stripped of all their disguises and bereft of all life's accomplishments, they feared to stand before God. To stand naked and alone before God was to stand without protection against God's anger.

But the anger of God is the wrath of the Lamb, and He Himself provides protection for His servants. The fact of His anger is the fact of His mercy too.

The Sealed Multitude 7:1-17

Let me, therefore, before I say any more about God's judgments, tell you what I saw as I looked at God's people in the midst of these judgments. I am now talking about those whose names are in the scroll of Life and who have been purchased unto God by the Lamb. I saw them as they were on the earth—those who in each generation keep their faith and make their witness amidst life's tribulation; I saw them also as they were in heaven—those who in all generations God had gathered to Himself, leading them through repentance to faith.

What was their secret of faith? It was that they who committed themselves to God's keeping were kept by Him. They were certainly not granted shelter. All that happened on the earth happened to them too. But nothing was able to separate them from the love of God in Christ Jesus their Lord.[33] They were as those who were sealed.[34] God had put the mark of His possession upon them.[35]

Four angels stood at the four corners of the earth restraining the four winds that cause destruction on the earth and on the sea and in the air. And, as these calamities were held in leash, I saw the servants of God sealed to be kept. The angel of light and hope who ascended from the rising of the sun called with a loud voice to the four angels at the four corners of the earth saying: "Do not harm the earth or the sea or the air till we have sealed the servants of our God upon their foreheads with the seal of the living God which is

[32] Isa. 2:19; Luke 23:30.
[33] Rom. 8:39.
[34] Eph. 1:13.
[35] Gal. 6:17.

His Holy Spirit." They that were sealed were God's people,[36] His true Israel. Indeed, they were so truly Israel that the names of Israel's tribes are their fitting symbol.[37] And of them there were twelve times twelve hundred, the number of completeness, for of His people God forgets not one.[38]

But this distinction between the sons of God and the children of earth in the midst of life's tribulation is only an immediate distinction. Ultimately the mercy of God's judgments is His will that all men must repent.[39] At least, as I looked into heaven I saw there what must finally come to pass: A great multitude which no man could number, from every nation, from all tribes and peoples and tongues, standing before the throne and before the Lamb. They were clothed in white robes and they had palm branches in their hands, and they cried with a great voice saying:[40]

"Saved by our God who is,
who is seated on the throne,
and by the Lamb."

And, at their cry, the angels of heaven fell down and worshiped saying:

"Amen!
Blessing and glory,
and wisdom and thanksgiving,
and honor and power and might,
be to our God forever and ever. Amen."

One of the ancients said to me, "Do you realize what it is you are seeing?" And I said, "Sir, you know." And he said, "These are they who have come out of the great tribulation; they have washed their robes and made them white in the blood of the Lamb."

The great tribulation! That certainly meant the persecution in which we were caught. But it also meant that constant tribulation of

[36] II Cor. 1:22; Ezek. 9:4-6.
[37] In John's list of the twelve tribes, Judah comes first, and Manasseh takes the place of the apostate Dan (Judg. 18:30).
[38] Gen. 49:1-33.
[39] Acts 17:30.
[40] Matt. 13:43; Phil. 3:21.

life which was the result of evil's warring against God. Out of that tribulation, and because of it, come the host of the redeemed.

Therefore are they before the throne of God, and serve Him day and night within His temple; and He who sits upon the throne will shelter them[41] with His presence.

They shall hunger no more, neither thirst any more; the sun shall not strike them, nor any scorching heat.

For the Lamb in the midst of the throne will be their shepherd, and He will guide them to springs of living water; and God will wipe away every tear from their eyes.

The. Unsealed Scroll *8:1*

The community of the "kept" on earth, the community of the "redeemed" in heaven—when I had understood this I was able also to understand the purpose of God for His Church in the world. I saw clearly that it was as the seals of time were broken and God's judgments, one by one, overtook the earth, that the sons of God stood increasingly distinguished from the rest of men.[42] They stood distinguished by their unshaken confidence in God's love—they were as those who were sealed; they also stood distinguished by the repentance with which they responded to His judgments—they were as those who were washed; until they became identifiable, distinguished from the rest, a distinct community, who by their manifest presence both hurried God's judgments to their culmination[43] and witnessed to God's invitation to men to repent.

We do not hear truly, within the Church, what the judgments of God declare as they come upon the earth unless we hear them as God's call for "the Remnant" to be gathered and for its testimony to be borne.

How did this revelation of the sons of God take place, and in what manner did I see it? I saw it happen as the seventh seal was broken and the scroll of Life was unrolled. Thereupon fell a great silence like the half-hour silence which intervenes between the blood offering and the offering of incense in the daily liturgy.[44] The redeemed com-

[41] Ps. 91:1.
[42] Matt. 5:14.
[43] Mark 13:20.
[44] Luke 1:10.

munity is redeemed by the shedding of blood; its task is to raise the incense of prayer.

The Altar in Heaven *8:2-5*

"Maran Atha"—Come, Lord Jesus: that is always the Church's supplication. The cherubim have called "Come," and four horsemen have appeared. The martyrs have cried "How long!" and the earth was shaken to its foundations. Now, the cry that issues in judgment is the cry of the Church at prayer.

There was the altar of intercession above and the altar of sacrifice below; and as heaven itself was hushed into silence the prayers of the saints ascended from earth to heaven.[45] There they mingled with the incense of prayer on heaven's altar. The worship of earth and of heaven was made one. And then, as the angel cast on the earth the fire with which this sacrifice of prayer had been consumed, there issued peals of thunder, loud noises, flashes of lightning, and a earthquake.[46]

What did these symbolize? They symbolized the effective sovereignty of God on earth, even as when they happened on Mount Sinai they symbolized the establishment of God's rule over His people.

The world rocks to its foundations and God's people are at prayer. It is their one form of direct participation in the rule of God. It is also the only way of keeping faith and loyalty secure when God's judgments are abroad upon the earth. Indeed, the consequence of His judgments is to help the world to see that there is in its midst a distinct community who, while sharing its ills, do not share its rebellion.

The Four Trumpets *8:6-12*

God's rule of a world in revolt must necessarily be exercised in judgment, but always mercy contends that judgment be held in restraint. Besides, throughout the course of judgment, the people of God are at prayer for the world, the quality of their life in the midst of judgment also witnessing to the world concerning the upholding grace of God.

[45] Ps. 141:2.
[46] Exod. 19:16; Rev. 8:5; 11:19; 16:18.

The seals of time have been broken, the scroll of Life has been unrolled,[47] and now it is the last hour, the hour of time's fulfillment, of the final call to repentance. Soon it will be "the close of the age" and the Son of Man will send His angels and they will gather out of His Kingdom all causes of sin and all evildoers, and throw them into the furnace of fire; but the righteous will shine like the sun.[48]

Listen to me as I tell you how I saw these things come to pass. I saw seven angels, and to each was given a trumpet; and as the first four angels blew their trumpets, destruction fell on the various necessities of life. Hail and blood-red rain, erupting volcano and falling meteors, and eclipses of sun and moon—these resulted in a destruction of fruit (a third part of the trees was burned up); a destruction of drink (a third part of all waters was made bitter); and a destruction of light (a third part of the sun and moon and stars was darkened).

It is when the necessities of life are touched that men most realize that they are flesh, and are most tempted to think that their flesh is the important part of themselves. They need to learn, and the children of God are committed to teach them, that men do not live by bread alone. To live by bread is but one way of life, to live by the Word of God given to oneself is another way of life. And, by this Word of God, a person can live even when there is no bread.[49] God's Word spoken and received has sustaining power.

Now, you will understand why destruction fell on only "a third part." Even when sin brings forth its consequences, those consequences are circumscribed by the mercy of God. It is not destruction that God wills but discipline, not retribution but punishment. He desires not that any should perish but that all should repent and turn to Him.[50]

The Shout of the Eagle 8:13–9:21

But what happens when they do not repent? There is such a thing as the tragedy of pure evil. I have told you how sin works destruction on human life (the four horsemen). I have shown you how it fills the

[47] Dan. 12:1-4.
[48] Matt. 13:40-43.
[49] Luke 4:4.
[50] II Pet. 3:9.

soul with terror in the face of earthly insecurity (the great earthquake). I have explained to you how it dims the reality of eternal values in the experience of fleshly needs (the four trumpets). And now, what is left but to make plain the final nature of sin as that which destroys the soul. The story of judgment is over; what I shall now describe are "Woes."

I saw these woes come upon the earth as the last three trumpets were sounded, and at the sound of each trumpet an eagle poised in midheaven shouted the woe. The eagle is where a corpse is,[51] and what is man but a corpse if his soul be dead! But from each woe the people of God were safe, they were sealed. The woes were "to them that are of the earth."

> Woe, Woe, Woe
> to them that are of the earth;
> because of the trumpet blasts
> of the three angels who are yet to sound.

The first of these three trumpets was blown, and at that blast an angel descended to the earth and opened the shaft that led to the abyss where Satan dwells. And from the mouth of the shaft there issued dense smoke which darkened the sun and the air.

> The four horsemen had appeared at the call of the cherubim. It was God who had ordained that where man hated his brother, both should abide in death. It is by God's decree that sin is self-destructive.
>
> The earthquake had happened at the cry of the martyrs. It was God who had ordained that where men sought first their own security, to them must be revealed the temporariness of earthly life. It is by God's decree that all earth-based security is shattered.
>
> The four trumpets had sounded at the prayers of the saints. It was God who had ordained that where men were satisfied with what the earth could give, they should also have the chance to learn how to live by God's word alone. It is by God's decree that materialism is hollow.
>
> But the woes which destroy the soul came not from God but from the abyss. They took place at the cry of a vulture.

[51] Luke 17:37.

How did I see the first woe? First as smoke from the abyss which darkened the soul, and then the soul itself athrob with pain. The judgments of God intend that men should repent, but when these judgments evoke not repentance but bitterness then the destruction of the soul has begun. Repentance is the only way of transmuting punishment into discipline,[52] but instead of doing this, men allow their souls, in the face of accumulating calamity, to be invaded by bitterness and doubt. In bitterness God's love is questioned, and in doubt God's sovereignty is impugned.[53]

What were they like, these twin agents of the abyss which I saw? They were as destructive as locusts eating away the joy of human life. They were as poisonous as scorpions causing the soul to pulse with pain. They were kingly, for when harbored they assumed control over all life's perspectives. They appeared human and seemingly reasonable but were as enticing as women's hair. They destroyed as lions destroy, they were as resistless as those clad in armor. They were the Devil's vanguard in his war against faith, the Devil whose name is Abaddon which means "Ruin."

The first woe has passed;
behold, two woes are still to come.

The natural result of doubt is apostasy, and of bitterness the casting away of all restraint. Ethical values lose their sanction, and there is nothing to prevent man from reverting to the law of the jungle. Besides, one of the results of the dislocation of life in the wake of war and natural disaster is that some men exploit the situation to prey upon their fellows. All this is the second woe. The first woe lasts only for a short time, for five months; the second woe follows quickly.

I looked, and behold I saw, as the second trumpet of the three was blown, a great army of horsemen sweep from across the Euphrates. I was reminded of the invasion of the Parthian hordes. They were two hundred million strong, and four angels went before them. These angels had been bound at the river but were now let loose.

Was not the Euphrates the crisis of Israel's pilgrimage? It was from beyond it that Abraham came when he was called by God.[54]

[52] Luke 13:3.
[53] Rom. 2:4.
[54] Gen. 24:6; Josh. 24:2.

But lo, the forces dammed off by that initial calling and dedication have broken through. Here was the reversal of the initial obedience, here was apostasy, here was even a reversion to the life of the animal.

Bitterness and doubt had been poisonous in their effects, but apostasy and lawlessness were ruinous also in themselves. Their power was both in their mouths and in their tails. The former merely tortured the soul, these latter led out the soul into ways of death. In their lawlessness men destroyed each other. Destructive also were the untruths which proceeded out of their mouths, lies about God and man and the world which seared the soul as fire, and blinded it as smoke and scorched it as brimstone.

The second woe has passed;
behold, the third woe is soon to come.

There is one end when the soul has apostatized, and that is eternal death. The angel will blow the third blast, and the time will come "for the dead to be judged and for destroying the destroyers of the earth."[55] That is the third woe. But the third woe was not yet; there was still time to repent.

And yet men repented not! In the face of judgment they felt qualms of conscience but no true desire for amendment of life; even when overwhelmed with terror they sought escape in hysterical religionism rather than in real penitence. They continued worshiping demons or idols, and working violence upon one another.

The sin of man is of two kinds: sin against God and sin against man. The sin against God consists in the worship of the work of one's hands. These may be either those powers (like humanity, family, race, nation, state, church, economic order) which have a right over the human spirit, but in exalting which to godhead men make them demons; or these may be those things (like wealth, position, power, influence, security) which men turn into idols, their substitutes for God. Sin against man consists in violence done to another's body—murder; or to another's mind—sorcery; or to another's soul—sexual vice; or to another's property—theft. But from all sin God demands repentance, and still waits for it.

[55] Rev. 11:18.

The Gospel of Redemption 10:1–11:11

The nature of God's demand for repentance, however, is seriously misunderstood if we think of it merely as arising from man's experience of God's judgments. Those who do not believe are rarely led to believe by any experience of disaster. Only they repent who perceive the connection between the judgments of God and His gospel of redemption.[56]

Lest, therefore, in speaking of judgment, I have left unstressed the gospel of redemption, listen to what I saw as I meditated upon this gospel.

I saw it in the guise of a strong angel coming down out of heaven arrayed with a cloud and with a rainbow over his head. The rainbow was the symbol given to Noah that God would be patient with the sons of men. The rainbow was over the throne of God.[57] Here I saw it also over the head of the angel who carried the open scroll.[58] The gospel is the open secret of God's mercy. Its radiance is never clouded, the angel's face was as the sun; its message is unwearied, the angel's feet were as pillars of fire.

And I saw the angel descend from heaven to earth. He planted his right foot on the sea and his left foot upon the earth, and he uttered a shout like a lion's roar. That shout was heard above the din and tumult of all earth's happenings. It proclaimed mercy over land and sea.

But mercy is not the postponement of judgment. To think of it in that way is to forget that, in the presence of God, man is always at the moment of decision. First the judgment of seals, then the judgment of trumpets, why not another series—a judgment of thunders, and so on? The angel said, "Write them not, for there shall be no more delay." The Master tarries but He will also come; so that it is precisely when He tarries that the message is declared, "Behold He comes."[59]

[56] Heb. 12:8.
[57] Rev. 4:3; Gen. 9:8-17; Eph. 3:1-13.
[58] There is an unopened scroll to be unrolled, but already there is an open scroll to be accepted. God's work of salvation has been done, and it is open to all to receive.
[59] Matt. 25:5-6; 24:48.

The end-event of His arrival is not simply an event at the end of time. The message of that event is proclaimed always,[60] "There shall be no more delay but, when the seventh angel shall sound, the mystery of God's delays shall be over and the gospel will come to its fulfillment."

I was bidden to make this message my own. The voice that had spoken to me spoke again and said, "Go, take the open scroll in the hand of the angel and eat it."[61] And, even as the angel warned me, I found the scroll sweet as honey in my mouth, but in my stomach it was bitter to digest. The gospel of redemption is sweet, but its process of fulfillment is bitter indeed. How bitter, only they know who have tried to witness to the gospel amidst the conflicts of the world. And mine was the task of witnessing to it and to its working amidst peoples and nations and languages and kings.[62]

This is the calling of the Church—to witness to the gospel of redemption. But, here again, the determining fact is the way in which God abides with His Church. Let me explain in terms of what I saw and what happened to me.

A measuring rod like a staff was given to me and I was told, "Rise and measure the temple of God and the altar and those who worship there, but do not measure the court outside the temple; leave that out."[63] The whole temple was not protected. The Church was at the mercy of the nations, and they trample it. And yet, through the whole period of conflict, the Church's witness to God was not silenced. His witnesses witnessed to Him clothed in sackcloth, the symbol of the sorrow in His heart and in their own. It seemed to me that the conflict raged for forty-two months, a period of time burned upon our memory because it was forty-two months that Antiochus Epiphanes maintained in the temple of Jerusalem an image of Olympian Zeus. Yet, God's double witness to Himself was always maintained.

There was the witness of "Law," the witness to God's eternal nature and changeless purpose. There was also the witness of "Prophecy," the witness to His activity of self-revelation. "The wages of sin is

[60] Rom. 16:25, 26.
[61] Ezek. 2:8–3:3.
[62] Jer. 1:10.
[63] When Jerusalem was besieged by Titus, the pious Jew spoke of the temple and the altar as having been measured by God for protection.

death," but God's love has been revealed in that "while men were yet sinners Christ died for the ungodly."[64]

Pharaoh tried to destroy Moses, but Moses had power to bring down plagues upon Egypt.[65] Ahab tried to destroy Elijah, but Elijah had power to shut up the heavens. Even so was God's witness empowered to maintain itself against all attack. God's witness is such that when men devise evil against it that evil simply turns upon them.

This does not mean that we should expect a literal repetition of the kind of marvels wrought by Moses and Elijah, but that we should not forget that there will be marvels, signs of the residence of God's power in His Church. God's witness is always accompanied by a manifestation of the powers of His Kingdom.[66]

Just as Zerubbabel and Joshua were witnesses to God in a country that lay in ruins, and because of their faithfulness rebuilt out of those ruins and upon them the splendor of a new Jerusalem, so will God's witnesses be. They will be like two lamps, unquenchably alight, each fed with oil from a living olive tree.

But God's redeeming purpose is not achieved simply by the maintenance of the Church's witness to Him and to His holy action in Jesus Christ. There also takes place in the life of the Church that fellowship in the sufferings of Christ for another's sake, by which is completed that which remains of His afflictions.[67]

Thus I saw the witnesses, when their hour had come and their testimony was accomplished, slain by the beast from the abyss. And their dead bodies lay in the street of the great city where also their Lord was crucified.

The world is like Jerusalem, God's holy city.[68] It is God's even when it is in rebellion and under the sway of men. It is Jerusalem even when it is Sodom and Egypt, even when it is drunk with sin and blind with cruelty and power.

And because it is Jerusalem, God's world,[69] Calvary is never final. Indeed, even the period of unmitigated evil is short. It lasts only for

[64] Rom. 5:6, 8.
[65] Exod. 7:19; I Kings 17:1; cf. II Kings 1:10.
[66] Mark 16:20.
[67] Col. 1:24.
[68] Rev. 11:2.
[69] Ps. 48:2.

three-and-a-half days compared to the three-and-a-half years of witness: albeit days of stark tragedy, with God's witness silent in death, its unburied corpse speaking vainly to men's dead souls, while the men themselves make merry and congratulate each other on the freedom they have achieved from the torment of God's insistent search for them.[70]

And then, Easter. For, though it is the beast from the abyss which destroys the two witnesses, the key of that abyss is with God, and God's redeeming work goes forward meeting every Calvary with Easter morning.

The Last Trumpet 11:12-19

"If we have become united with Him by the likeness of His death, we shall be also by the likeness of His resurrection."[71] This is the Church's abiding experience. It is also the foretaste of the end-event.

The meaning of the resurrection experience lies in the past. It lies in the resurrection of Jesus Christ. The song which I heard the ancients sing was a song of His triumph then and of His triumph ever afterward. It was the constant song of heaven as they celebrated the reign of Christ upon the earth. They celebrated His victory. "We give thanks to Thee," they sang, "Lord God almighty, who art and who wast;[72] that Thou hast taken Thy great power and begun to reign." They celebrated His effective sovereignty maintained against all rebellion. "The nations raged but Thy wrath came, and came also the time of judgment." They celebrated His judgment as He executes it in history: "His judgment of those who are dead in their sins; His judgment of His servants, His prophets and His saints; and His judgment of those who are the violent men of the earth."

So does the meaning of the resurrection experience lie also in the present. For, since Jesus Christ is Lord, His resurrecting power abides for His Church.[73] I saw the two witnesses whom the beast had slain stand upon their feet, for the breath of life from God entered into

[70] Amos 8:11.
[71] Rom. 6:5.
[72] The phrase "who is to come" is here absent because by the end of chapter 11 the story has reached its climax. He who is to come has come. Chapter 12 begins a new section.
[73] Here is the same truth about the millennial reign of the martyr church which finds extended treatment in Rev. 20:1-6.

them, and they went up to heaven and the world was struck with fear.

Whenever the risen power of Christ is made manifest it causes fearful surprise.[74] The oppressed Church shows again that it is in Christ in the heavenly places, and the oppressors are dumfounded; while the earth itself tastes the fruits of its own rebellion. Cannot you remember that so it happened to Jerusalem? The Church spread, but the city where the Lord was crucified was struck down. Titus and his legions came like an earthquake and killed seven thousand persons, destroying, of the city, a complete tenth.

May not fear sometimes be the cause of turning men's minds to God! At least, so it seemed to me. For in my vision I saw those who were not destroyed being sore afraid, and in their fear giving glory to the God of heaven.

But, the resurrection experience is not only past and present, it is future too. For both past and present point to that final event when the cycle of judgment shall be complete and the third woe come; when God's redeeming work shall have reached fulfillment and the last trumpet be sounded.

The seventh angel sounded his trumpet and there was heard in heaven the shout of the heavenly host:

"The kingdom of the world has become
the kingdom of our Lord and of His Christ,
and He shall reign forever and ever."

Then the ancients fell on their faces and worshiped God, replying with the song of celebration:

"We give thanks to Thee, Lord God almighty, who art and who wast,
that Thou hast taken Thy great power and begun to reign.
The nations raged, but Thy wrath came,
and the time for the dead to be judged,
for rewarding Thy servants, the prophets and saints,
and those who fear Thy name, both small and great,
and for destroying the destroyers of the earth."

Then was thrown open the temple of God in heaven, and the ark of His covenant was seen within His temple.[75] There was also seen on earth the manifest signs of the rule of the Christ.

[74] Acts 4:13.
[75] Heb. 9:1-2.

The Unveiling of God's Power

The rule of God is the rule of One who sits enthroned amidst the worship of earth and of heaven. His throne is inside a temple. God's temple in heaven was opened, and the ark of His covenant was seen.

I have already written of the Lord of the Church, Him whom I saw amidst the lampstands. I have already written of the Lord of the world, Him whom I saw amidst the throne. I now write of the Lord of all rule, Him whom I saw within His temple. The earthly ark was the symbol of God's faithfulness to our fathers; the heavenly ark is the symbol of His faithfulness to us.

What is the purpose of God's rule, and how is His power exercised? It is exercised in judgment and mercy, calling men to repentance and faith; it is also exercised in condemnation of evil, every form of evil being contested and destroyed. It is of this contest in our own time that I now write to you. The strife in which we are engaged is not simply a strife between the Church and the imperial power of Rome; rather, it is another phase of the age-long conflict between God and Satan—"the unseen power that controls this dark world, and spiritual agents from the very headquarters of evil."[1] Indeed, the struggle in which we are involved is a decisive phase, it may even be the last phase; but He must reign until all God's enemies are subdued. Only then will the Kingdom come, the Kingdom of the Father, who at the end will be all in all.[2]

The Dragon against the Child 12:1-17

When God made the world, He made man in His own image. Men were to be His sons. This original creation itself was a conflict between light and darkness. The dragon of darkness had to be pierced that light might shine forth.[3] Nevertheless, darkness itself was not dissolved. Always, light shines forth and darkness contends with it.[4]

Similar was the sign that I saw in heaven. I saw a woman arrayed with the sun, with the moon under her feet, and with a crown of

[1] Eph. 6:12, Phillips.
[2] I Cor. 15:25-28.
[3] Job 26:13.
[4] John 1:5.

twelve stars upon her head; and she was with child.[5] (Remember that Israel was made up of the children of the twelve patriarchs, and that twelve disciples were our Lord's first constitution of His Church.)[6] But ranged against the woman who was with child was a great, red dragon. It had its followers too, a third part of the stars of heaven. Evil contests the purpose of God to bring forth sons unto glory.[7] I saw this contest on earth as a struggle between the dragon and the woman's child, I saw the contest in heaven as a struggle between the dragon and Michael, God's servant.

The dragon watched and waited; but when the woman delivered her child, the child was caught up to God and unto His throne; while the dragon was cast down to earth and his angels with him. The great deceiver was unmasked.

But, as I saw it, the battle for "dominion" was not over; Satan's desire was still to make all rule subservient to him; so that, even though the Son of Mary had won the victory, both on earth and in heaven the battle still raged. The dragon was cast down but he was yet alive, and he persecuted the woman still, and all her seed.

But you, in the midst of this conflict, also know the consequences of the victory of Christ already won. The dragon has already received its death wound, and its wrath is only for a short time.[8] Tribulation is only for three-and-a-half years. Besides, even during this period the Church is kept in peace by the victory of Christ. It is carried, as if on eagle's wings, into the wilderness and there kept safe against the day when it will inherit the promised land.[9] The accuser is unable anymore to accuse. It is God that justifies.

Thus it was that even while the dragon renewed on earth its war with God and with God's children, I heard already in heaven the shout of victory:

[5] The story of the goddess who was destined to bear a son who would rule the world, and was pursued by a dragon when she was about to bring forth was an international myth in the ancient world (Gen. 3:15).

[6] Acts 7:38; Gal. 4:26.

[7] Heb. 2:10.

[8] Luke 10:18; John 12:31.

[9] Exod. 9:4; Jer. 2:2; Hos. 2:2-7.

"Now it has come,
the salvation and power,
the reign of our God and the authority of His Christ.
For he is cast down—
the accuser of our brethren—
who accused them before God day and night.
"But they have conquered him
by the blood of the Lamb and the Word to which they testify;
they had to die for it but they did not cling to life.
Rejoice for this, O heavens,
and ye that dwell in them."[10]

And yet, and yet, even though the final victory is sure, the immediate conflict is still terrible. The certainty of triumph cannot altogether hide anxiety concerning the strife. It was on this note of anxiety that I heard the shout of heaven end:

"Alas to you, O earth and sea,
for the Devil has come down to you in great wrath,
because he knows that his time is short."

The first thing which I saw the dragon do, however, was not to engage in any conflict as such. It tried simply to drown its enemy in a flood of lies. It tried to confuse the issues. But, as always, false teaching comes to nought. Earth itself swallows it up. The very structure of creation is against it, and it is soon exposed. An open fight between God and evil is inevitable.

Of what nature is this fight? Let me answer in terms of the symbols of evil which I saw.

The Four Monsters *13:1-10; 17:1-18*

The first symbol was the abyss monster. I have already shown you this symbol in my account of how God's witnesses were attacked. The abyss is restless chaos out of which God wrested the world by the power of His Word. And it remains beneath the world which God so wrested, a rebellious force beating its will against the will of God.[11]

[10] The concept of a precosmic fall was of gradual growth among the Jewish thinkers. It was a further attempt to answer the question, "Whence and what is sin?" (Ezek. 28:11-17; Isa. 24:21; II Pet. 2:4.)

[11] Gen. 1:2; Job 7:12; Rev. 9:2.

The second symbol was the raging dragon. The Babylonians spoke of darkness as a dragon (Tiamat) with which the god of light (Marduk) had to wrestle at the dawn of creation; and our fathers in Israel spoke of Egypt as a dragon (Rahab) with which Yahweh had to contend in order to set His people free.[12] As I saw it, it was still as a raging dragon that evil attacked the holy purposes of God.

The third symbol was the horn-crowned beast. Here was the very caricature of the Lamb. "The Lamb was and is and is to come"; the beast, on the other hand, "was and is not and is to come." "It is not" because the Devil has been dethroned, and yet how terribly true that always "it is to come."[13] The Lamb had seven horns and seven eyes; the beast had seven heads and ten horns.[14] Evil has no eyes. Also, just as the Lamb was the Lamb that was slain, so was the beast. It carried a mortal wound. It received it in its contest with Jesus.

It is this same beast with which we contend in our own time. Look how "Rome" looms up across the sea, its form that of a leopard cruel in its strength, its feet those of a bear heavy in its tread, and its mouth that of a devouring lion. When Nero died, Rome seemed to be doomed with weaklings in power; and yet today, under the strong rule of the Flavians, that wound has been healed. Rome is as secure as ever. In fact, she and her emperors are now demanding worship. The beast that I saw carried diadems on its horns, and names of blasphemy on its heads—Augustus, Divus, Dominus. Also, the people acknowledged these claims and gave the beast idolatrous worship.

But I saw also this difference, that only "they that dwelt upon the earth" worshiped the beast; whereas "they who tabernacled in heaven" refused to worship it. It is these whose names were written in the scroll of Life of the Lamb. Against these the beast made war. For forty-two months it could oppress them, and during that time it could even claim that the power it had was that of the dragon itself. "The kingdoms of the world are mine" is always the claim of Satan,[15] and Satan gives his authority to whomsoever will fall down and wor-

[12] Job 26:12, 13; Ezek. 29:3-6.
[13] I Cor. 2:6, Moffatt.
[14] Rev. 5:6.
[15] Luke 4:6.

ship him. We can see how, in our time, he has given his authority to Rome.

The fourth symbol of evil, therefore, was Rome herself. I saw a bacchanal borne upon a beast. She was "Rule" and "Power"; and the beast was the kingdoms of the world, with each of its heads representing one kingdom. The pretensions of men find their final form in the kingdoms of the world, and these kingdoms tempt men to worship worldly power. The woman robed with light was the mother of sons unto glory; the woman robed in the purple of power and the scarlet of sin was a harlot and the mother of adulterers. The kings of the earth commit fornication with her, and "they that dwell in the earth" drink the wine of her fornication. She was arrayed in purple and scarlet and decked with precious stones, while in her hand was a cup full of abominations. And on her forehead was her name:

MYSTERY
Babylon the Great
the mother of adultery[16]
and of the abominations of the earth.[17]

Why "mystery"? Because of the mystery of evil. Why "Babylon"? Because Babylon was God's instrument of judgment on Israel as well as the land in which the people of God were held captive.[18] The woman was drunk with the blood of the saints and with the blood of the martyrs of Jesus.

As for the beast that carried this bacchanal, it had names of blasphemy written on its body, and it had seven heads and ten horns. Of the seven heads, five had fallen—the five which in the past had held captive the people of God: Egypt, Assyria, Babylon, Persia, Greece—the sixth, which was the reigning head, was Rome, and there was still a seventh whose kingdom was to come.

Of the seventh, what shall I say? You know the general expectation that soon Parthia will overtake Rome, and that with the Parthian hordes Nero himself will return from the abyss.[19] If so, the Parthian

[16] Most ancient Latin manuscripts read "mother of adultery." Roman prostitutes wore their names in the fillet which encircled their brows.

[17] Nah. 3:4; Isa. 23:16-17.

[18] Jer. 51:6-10.

[19] In the year 68, nearly thirty years before John wrote his book, Nero had committed suicide, forsaken by his bodyguard, as a powerful rival with an army was approaching Rome. Soon a legend grew up that he was not dead but would return; or, if dead, would return from the abyss.

kingdom will last only for a little while to be succeeded by an eighth head. However, the kingdom of Nero redivivus will not strictly be an eighth kingdom. It will simply be the final manifestation of all the seven heads, the manifestation of naked power in its stark cruelty and in its total revolt against God. With Nero are expected to rule the satraps of Parthia, the ten horns, but that will be just for an hour. Time is getting short and the end is near.

Will that be the final end? Every end is final. But here I speak of the end that will come to Rome:

> she who sits on the seven mountains
> and rules over the kings of the earth,
> whose dominion extends over peoples
> and multitudes and nations and tongues.

The harlot will be destroyed by the very beast which carries her, the returning Nero from the abyss will himself lay her low. By evil shall evil be brought down.[20] So will the purposes of God find fulfillment, and His words be accomplished.

And then? And then the beast itself will be overcome by the Lamb.

> For He is Lord of lords and King of kings,
> and those with Him are called and chosen and faithful.

Let not the certainty of this outcome, however, create in you a false hope of present security. For, as long as the conflict lasts, the saints of God are at the mercy of the beast. There will be no divine intervention to save them from all that may happen to them.[21]

> If any man is for captivity, into captivity he goes;
> if any man is to be killed with the sword, with the
> sword he must be killed.

Here is a call for the endurance and faith of the saints.

It is to support your endurance and faith that I write. Remember your true situation and stand fast. I remind you again that though you are engaged in this conflict on earth your true situation is that of worshipers in heaven. There your prayers are offered at the heavenly altar. Satan makes war on them who "tabernacle in heaven," while God seeks to win for himself those who are "dwellers upon earth."[22]

[20] Ezek. 16:1-63; 23:1-49.
[21] Luke 23:31.
[22] Rev. 8:4; 11:10.

The Mark of the Beast and of the Lamb 13:11–14:5

Thus, while, on the one hand, you are the company of those who on earth refuse to be branded with the mark of the emperor; on the other hand, you are those who stand in heaven, the company of those who bear the name of the Lamb written on their foreheads. When you suffer, therefore, for your refusal to be branded with the mark of the beast, remember your share in the triumph of heaven.

It is not easy for you, that I know. For not only do you face the edict of the beast, but you face also the authority of a second beast who seeks in so many ways to implement that edict. The first beast is Rome whose power is exercised from across the sea, but the second beast is native to your land. It is, as you know, the local priesthood. Their priestly headdress has two horns reminding you of a lamb; but they speak not of the Lamb, nor like one, but as a dragon. Their function is to make "the dwellers of earth" worship the beast.

They do this in many ways. They seek, first of all, to win men's credulity by so-called miracles: causing fire to come down from heaven, and making the statue of the beast to speak. They seek also to evoke men's adulation by recounting to them the story of the empire and its recovery from its death stroke. But, more than this, they set up images of the beast in many parts of the land and put to the sword those who refuse to offer worship to it.

But those who do offer worship are acknowledged with a brand mark. It is a mark which is both a number and a name, and the number is also the number of the name. He that has understanding will understand, for the number is six hundred and sixty-six.

Roman soldiers often brand themselves with the name of their general.[23] Why not, then, those who worship the emperor? Already, there is the "charagma," the official seal of the emperor, giving his name and the year of his reign, which is necessary for all legal documents relating to buying and selling. How convenient, therefore, that this charagma should be branded either on the right hand or on the forehead of those who have worshiped the beast, and that it should be decreed that only those who had this mark could either buy or sell.

[23] Gal. 6:17.

The ordinary intercourse of life has been made for you dependent on apostasy.

But, as you consider this situation in which you stand, I want you also to see what I saw: the Lamb standing on Mount Zion and with Him the one hundred forty-four thousand, sealed on earth[24] but already triumphant in heaven.[25] There broke over them like thunder, or as the waves breaking on the shore, the sound of many harps, and a song was raised before the throne and before the cherubim and the ancients. It was the new song of heaven, the song of redemption, and only they who had been purchased out of the earth, even the one hundred forty-four thousand, knew it. These are they who follow the Lamb whithersoever He goes, even to Calvary. In their mouth is no lie, nor have they committed fornication. They have kept their hearts virgin against the coming of their Lord. They are the first fruits of mankind, redeemed for God and for the Lamb.[26]

This is your heavenly destiny. Forget it not, neither forget that what you are in heaven is what you are already on earth.

Four Harvest Cries 14:6-13

I have paused to explain to you the full significance of the conflict of our time. Let me now press on with the rest of my vision which is about the final end, the final outcome of the struggle between God and evil. "Let the wheat and tares grow together," the Master has said, "but when harvest comes, the wheat shall be reaped and garnered, the tares shall be reaped and burned."[27] At the end of every age, harvest must come; at the close of every crisis, the consequences must be reaped.

When the harvest takes place, it will be a harvest of repentance.

I saw an angel flying in midheaven, with an eternal gospel[28] to

[24] The Hebrew of the passage in Ezek. 9:4 suggests that the mark made was the Hebrew letter "*tau*" (Torah—law). The form of this letter, in Ezekiel's time and in John's, was that of the Greek letter "*chi*" (X) which was the Christian symbol for Christus (Χριστὸς).

[25] Rev. 7:4.

[26] Isa. 1:18.

[27] Matt. 13:30.

[28] The gospel of God as Creator and Judge is eternal and universal. All men always face the demand of this gospel, irrespective of whether they have heard the gospel in Jesus Christ or not (Rom. 1:20).

> proclaim to those who dwell on earth, to every nation and tribe and tongue and people. "Fear God and give Him glory," he said, "for the hour of His judgment has come. Worship Him who made heaven and earth, the sea and the depths beneath the sea."

Both the judgments of God and the evidences that show this world to be His world are means whereby He is pleading with men that they repent and turn again to Him.

When the harvest takes place, it will be also a harvest of retribution.

> I saw a second angel which followed. He cried, "Fallen, fallen is Babylon the great, she who made all nations drink of the sins of her impure passion."

The judgment of God is a judgment of redemption, but that redemption means the very destruction of evil. Every false love and every false lover will be destroyed.[29]

When the harvest takes place, it will be a harvest of remorse too.

> A third angel followed saying with a loud voice, "They that have drunk from the hands of Babylon the wine of her impure passion will drink also from the hands of God the wine of His wrath. From this wrath there is no escape. They will constantly be in the presence of the Lamb and of His holy angels, a presence that will be their torment."

They that worship the Lamb rest not day or night, neither is there rest for those who have worshiped the beast.[30] The saints will understand what this means, and bravely persevere in keeping the commandments of God and the faith of Jesus.

When the harvest takes place, it will be finally a harvest unto rest.

> I heard a voice from heaven saying, "Write this: Blessed are the dead who die in the Lord henceforth." "Blessed indeed," says the Spirit, "that they may rest from their labors, for their deeds follow them."

At the end of judgment is the great day of Sabbath when the Lord shall have completed His work and His people will enter into their rest.[31]

The Harvest Is Reaped *14:14-20*

Then I looked, and lo, a white cloud, and seated on the cloud one like a Son of Man, with a golden crown on His head, and a sharp

[29] Rev. 2:22.
[30] Rev. 4:8.
[31] Heb. 4:9.

sickle in His hand. And an angel came out of the temple, the temple from which all God's judgments proceed, and he called with a loud voice to Him who sat upon the cloud, "Put in your sickle, and reap, for the hour to reap has come, for the harvest of the earth is fully ripe."[32] So He who sat upon the cloud swung His sickle on the earth, and the earth was reaped.

Then came, out of the temple in heaven, another angel, and he too had a sharp sickle. He was the angel of God's wrath, and he waited for the cry of the angel that kept the altar on earth beneath which the blood of the martyrs was poured. And when this angel cried with a loud voice, "Put in your sickle and gather the clusters of the vine of the earth, for its grapes are ripe," the harvesting angel swung his sickle on the earth and gathered its vintage and threw it into the great wine press of the wrath of God.[33] And, when the wine press was trodden, blood flowed from it.

So takes place the double harvesting of our world. The Son of Man gathers all men to judgment, while at the same time the deeds of men as the architects of history are subjected to God's decisive will. However, He who trod the wine press had trodden it before—outside the city—and His wrath overflows in shedding His own blood.[34]

The blood from the wine press rose as high as a horse's bridle and flowed over, covering the whole earth.[35]

The Bowls of Wrath and Song of Deliverance *15:1-8*

Then I saw another portent in heaven, great and wonderful, seven angels with seven bowls containing the seven plagues. These were the last, for with them the wrath of God was ended.

But even as I saw these seven angels and what they signified, I thought of you. I gazed across the waters of the sea from where I stood and visualized you in your little churches. And, do you know what happened? It seemed to me that the sea turned red, the setting sun touching it with fire, and I saw you on the further side standing as Israel must have stood after its deliverance across the Red Sea. And

[32] Mark 4:29.
[33] Matt. 13:41.
[34] Heb. 13:12.
[35] Two world wars within a twenty-five-year period, with their terrible shedding of blood, are an illustration of this figure of the wine press which John uses.

I heard you strike the harps of God and sing the song of deliverance, which is the song of Moses and of the Lamb.[36]

"Great and wonderful are Thy deeds,
O Lord God the Almighty!
Just and true are Thy ways,
O King of the ages!
Who shall not fear and glorify Thy name, O Lord?
For Thou alone art holy.
All nations shall come and worship Thee,
For thy judgments have been revealed."

I noticed too that while the temple of the tent of witness in heaven was open—the temple from which came the angels with the bowls—yet the temple was also filled with smoke from the glory of God and from His power so that no man could enter the temple until the seven plagues were ended.

In the temple are the tables of the Law bearing witness to God's uncompromising demands and inexorable justice.[37] In the temple is also the ark of God which is the symbol of His grace. In the midst of judgment no man can come to the ark nor is the ark visible, but when the smoke has lifted, men will see that the ark has been there and has been there all the time.

This is the victory by which we overcome the world, even our faith in His grace.[38]

The Four Plagues *16:1-9*

Then I heard a loud voice from the temple telling the angels, "Go and pour out on the earth the bowls of the wrath of God." We know the story of the plagues that Moses called down upon Egypt.[39] Now it is the story of the plagues as they fell on "Babylon."

The first angel went and poured his bowl on the earth, and foul and evil sores came upon the men who bore the mark of the beast and worshiped its image. The consequence of false worship is the festering of the soul.

The second angel poured his bowl into the sea, and the sea which

[36] Exod. 15:1-27.
[37] II Chron. 5:7-10.
[38] I John 5:4.
[39] Exod. 7:14 ff.

served the empire and all its needs became like the blood of a dead man, and every living thing died that was in the sea. Death is the end of all human pretensions.

The third angel poured his bowl into the rivers and the fountains of water, wherever the towns and cities were in which the beast was worshiped, and they became blood. "Just art Thou in these Thy judgments, Thou who art and wast, O Holy One. For men have shed the blood of saints and prophets, and Thou hast given them blood to drink. It is their due."

The fourth angel poured his bowl on the sun, and it was allowed to scorch men with fire; men were scorched by the fierce heat, and they cursed the name of God who had power over these plagues, but they did not repent or give Him glory. The warmth of power ends in being scorched by it.

But these plagues were only the beginning of the end, and judgment moved swiftly to the destruction of the beast itself.

The End of Evil 16:10-21

This is how I saw it. The fifth, sixth, and seventh angels poured out their bowls of wrath, and these fell on the very beast itself and on its throne and on its kingdom. Its followers gnawed their tongues in anguish and cursed the God of heaven, but would not repent of their deeds.

There was also a gathering for battle of all the kings of the earth on the hills of Megiddo. Here on the classic battleground of Israel, where so many of its great and decisive battles were fought, the kings of the earth fought against and destroyed one another.[40]

The Antitrinity of hell—the dragon, the beast, and the false prophet—have many agents. These croak about the greatness of their masters in the ears of the kings who listen to them, and, misled by the apparent success of one earth-bound imperialism, set out to build such empires for themselves. So they come into conflict with one another and destroy one another, as well as the world which they seek to master.

I saw also this battle as a battle between Rome and the kings of the east, the forces of Parthia. But more than all, I saw it as a battle be-

[40] Judg. 5:19; II Kings 23:29.

tween the armies of the beast and the followers of the Lamb. The end of evil is by self-destruction. It is also by the power of the greatness of God.

So it was done. God's rule was established. The beast was vanquished. Babylon was destroyed. And the sons of men who would not repent felt the force of God's anger.

The Judgment of Rome *18:1-8, 21-24*

After this, I saw another angel coming down from heaven, having great authority; and the earth was made bright with his splendor. And he called out with a mighty voice:

"Fallen, fallen is Babylon the great!
It has become a dwelling place of demons,
a haunt of every foul spirit,
a haunt of every foul and hateful bird;
for all nations have drunk the wine of her impure passion
and the kings of the earth have committed fornication with her,
and the merchants of the earth have grown rich with the wealth of her wantonness."

There will always be for you the temptation to think that God's judgment of Rome is His vengeance on Rome for the way in which she persecuted the saints. It is important to remember that Rome fell as a result of its own opulent power and the way in which she led the kings of the earth and the captains of business to commit adultery with forms of worldly rule. The harlotry of Jerusalem was apostasy. She left her rightful lord and committed adultery with other lovers.[41] The harlotry of Babylon is rivalry. She set herself up as an alternative to God and caused men and nations to commit adultery with her. Her sin was pride, pride in the face of God, and by that pride she fell.

I speak of Babylon not Rome, for Rome is simply the Babylon of our own time. Every Babylon has fallen, the Babylon of our own time will fall, and so it will be unto the end of time, until at the last the Lord has subdued all His enemies and put them all under His feet.[42]

[41] Rev. 11:8; 17:5.
[42] Ps. 110:1.

Here, therefore, in the very fate of Babylon, is also a warning to all God's people. I heard a voice from heaven saying:

"Come out of her, O my people,
that you share not her sins,
that you partake not of her punishment:
for high as heaven her sins are heaped,
and God calls her misdeeds to the reckoning.[43]

"Render to her what she rendered to others,
aye, double the doom for all she has done;
in the cup which she mingled, mingle her double.
as she gloried herself, and waxed wanton;
so give her like measure of torture and tears.[44]

"Since in her heart she vaunts, 'A queen I sit,
no widow I, tears I shall never know,'[45]
so shall her plagues fall in a single day,
pestilence, tears, and famine, and fire,
for strong is God the Lord her judge."

Then a mighty angel took up a stone like a great millstone and threw it into the sea saying:[46]

"So shall the great city, Babylon,
be hurled down hurtling,
  and never be seen anymore.[47]
and sound of harpists and minstrels
and fluteplayers and trumpeters
  shall never be heard in thee more:
and craftsmen of any craft
  shall never be found in thee more
and the sound of the millstone
  shall never be heard in thee more:
and the light of a lamp
  shall never be seen in thee more:

[43] Jer. 51:6, 45; II Cor. 6:17.
[44] Cf. Isa. 40:2.
[45] Isa, 47:7; Ezek. 27:3.
[46] Mark 9:42.
[47] Jer. 51:63.

and the voice of the bridegroom and bride
shall never be heard in thee more.

"Vanished the ripe fruit of thy soul's desire!
Perished thy luxury and splendor!
never again to be seen
For the magnates of earth were thy traders;
all nations were seduced by thy magic spells."

Lamentation *18:9-20; 19:1-4*

I also heard a great lamentation, lamentation for the beauty and the richness which were no more, lamentation by all who had profited from the sins of the city which now was being consumed by fire.[48]

The kings of the earth wept and wailed, they who had shared in the corrupting power that now had come to its doom. "Alas," they cried.

"Alas, thou great city,
thou mighty city, Babylon!
In one hour has thy judgment come."[49]

The great merchants also wept for there was no one anymore to buy their rich merchandise: gold, silver, jewels, pearls, fine linen, purple, silk, scarlet, scent, ivory, costly wood, bronze, iron, marble, cinnamon, spice, incense, myrrh, frankincense, wine, oil, fine flour, wheat, cattle, sheep, horses, chariots, slaves, the souls of men. These merchants had profited according to their desires by their trade in the great city, and now the city was no more. They cried: "Alas."

"Alas, for the great city
that was clothed in fine linen, in purple and scarlet,
bedecked with gold, with jewels, and with pearls!
In one hour all this wealth has been laid waste.

"The fruit for which thy soul longed has gone from thee,
and all thy dainties and thy splendor are lost to thee,
never to be found again."

And there was weeping which arose from the men whose work was

[48] Rev. 17:2.
[49] Isa. 47:7.

on the sea, shipmasters and seafaring men and sailors. "Alas," they cried.

"Alas, for the great city
where all who had ships at sea grew rich by her wealth!
In one hour she has been laid waste."

There was real sorrow in all this lamentation. The record of "power," even of "power" that has been proud and overweening, is not all bad. But not on its record of achievement as on itself will judgment be passed. "In her was found the blood of prophets and of saints, and of all who have been slain on earth."[50] Among the merchandise sold in her streets were the "souls of men."

"Rejoice over her, O heaven,
O saints and apostles and prophets
for God has given judgment for you against her!"

And I heard a great multitude in heaven reply:

"Hallelujah!
Salvation and glory and power are our God's!
True and just are His sentences of doom.[51]
He has doomed the great harlot who destroyed earth
with her vice,
He has avenged on her the blood of His servants.
Hallelujah!
The smoke of her goes up forever and ever."[52]

And the twenty-four elders and the four living creatures fell down and worshiped God who is seated on the throne, and said: "Amen, hallelujah."

The Great Hallelujah *19:5-16*

My vision now hurries to its close. The last Babylon has fallen, and I can see the people of God made ready against the coming of their King. I heard a voice come forth from the throne, and it said:

"Praise our God, all you his servants,
You who fear him, small and great."

And I heard a great multitude answer with a mighty voice like the

[50] Matt. 23:35.
[51] Rev. 16:7.
[52] Isa. 34:10.

sound of many waters and the sound of many thunderpeals:

" 'Hallelujah! For the Lord our God the Almighty reigns.
Let us rejoice and exult and give Him the glory,
for the marriage of the Lamb has come,
And His bride has made herself ready.[53]
It was granted her to be clothed
with fine linen, bright and pure—
for the fine linen is the righteous deeds of the saints."

The Bridegroom comes when the bride is ready, and yet it is also true that no one knows when the Bridegroom will come.[54] This double truth is simply the counterpart of that other double truth that, on the one hand, the bride of the Lamb is an earthly community cured by God of infidelity and perfected by His discipline; while, on the other hand, the bride comes down from God out of heaven prepared and adorned for her husband. At the end will be the union of the Bridegroom with His bride, at the end will also be the bridal feast when all God's children will sit at His banquet.[55]

"Blessed are those who are invited
to the marriage supper of the Lamb."

An angel said to me, "These are the true words of God"; Whereupon I fell down at his feet to worship him. But he forbade me. "I am a fellow servant," he said, "with you and your brethren who hold the testimony of Jesus, which testimony is the breath of all prophecy. Worship God."[56]

Then I saw heaven opened, and behold, a white horse! The Bridegroom arrives clad as a warrior, to wage war against the powers that have set themselves up against him and have sought to turn away from Him the worship of His bride.[57] He must first destroy them before He celebrates His union with her.

His name is "Faithful and True."
In righteousness He judges and makes war.
His eyes are like a flame of fire,
On His head are many diadems.

[53] Hos. 2:19; Isa. 54:5.
[54] Matt. 25:5.
[55] Matt. 22:1-10.
[56] Col. 2:18.
[57] Isa. 11:4.

There is a name written upon Him known only to Himself.
He is clad in a robe sprinkled with blood,
and the name by which He is called is the "Word of God."[58]
The armies of heaven follow Him on white horses,
they are arrayed in fine linen, white and pure.
From His mouth issues a sharp sword to smite the nations.[59]
He will rule them with a rod of iron,
He will tread the wine press of the fury of the
wrath of God the Almighty.
On His robe and on His thigh He has a name inscribed,
King of kings and Lord of lords.[60]

It is not only at the end, however, that the Lord will come. He comes every time that the Church is ready for him.

The Four Powers *19:17–20:6*

Every time that the Church sets herself free from her worldly alliances and faces without fear her lonelines for Christ's sake, she is visited by God with strength and endowed with power; and it is given to her to reign with Christ for a thousand years.[61]

This millennial reign is that period, long or short, during which the Church is entrusted with "rule" and influence at the close of her time of testing. For even as she shares in the fellowship of His sufferings she will share in the power of His resurrection.[62]

I can see such a period dawning for you to whom I write, for though your period of conflict is not yet over, I already see the birds gathering to devour the corpses of those who will fall by the sword of the rider on the white horse. This is the banquet of the beast.

I saw an angel standing in the sun, and with a loud voice he called to all the birds that fly in midheaven:

"Come, gather for the great supper of God,
to eat the flesh of kings, of captains, and mighty men,
the flesh of horses and their riders,
and the flesh of all men, free and slave, small and great."

[58] Isa. 63:1; John 1:1.
[59] Rev. 2:16.
[60] Deut. 10:17.
[61] II Tim. 2:12.
[62] Phil. 3:10.

And that was what happened. For the four powers—the dragon, the beast, the false prophet, and the kings of the earth with their armies—waged war against Him who rode upon the horse and upon His army, and were defeated. The beast and the false prophet who worked for the beast were thrown alive into the lake of fire that burns with brimstone, and there they were destroyed. The kings and their armies were slain with the sword and the birds gorged themselves on their flesh. The dragon was seized by an angel coming down from heaven, holding in his hand the key of the bottomless pit and a great chain. This angel bound the dragon, that ancient serpent who is the Devil and Satan, and threw him into the pit and shut it and sealed it over him.

Then I saw thrones, and seated on them were those to whom judgment was committed.[63] It was the reign of Christ, for Christ must reign till all God's enemies are subdued. So that His reign is manifested on earth not only in suffering love, not only in faith kept firm amidst temptation and persecution, not only in victory over the powers of evil, but also in periods of triumph where, with Him, His martyr church is renewed and exercises the power of His gospel—that gospel for which it had already suffered.

This is the first resurrection, the resurrection of the martyr church. The "souls" of the martyrs will live again. The second resurrection is the resurrection at the end of time when all shall be raised from the dead to be judged, some to inherit eternal life, others to be condemned to final death. But this second death has no power over those who have already died for Christ, and who have shared in the glory of the Church. They shall be priests of God and of Christ, and they shall reign with Him a thousand years.[64]

Gog and Magog *20:7-10*

But this thousand years must come to an end.[65] It always does. The struggle between good and evil, God and the Devil, the Church and the powers is renewed. Satan is released from his prison, and once again the peoples of the earth are seduced.

[63] I Cor. 6:2; Luke 19:12-27.
[64] Rom. 6:8-11.
[65] II Pet. 3:8.

Yes. But is there no final end? There is. It seemed to me, as I thought of it, that I saw "Gog and Magog" (to use the names which the prophet Ezekiel used to describe the permanent enemies of Israel)[66] gather themselves for the last battle. Their number was like the sand of the sea. And they marched up over the broad earth and surrounded the camp of the saints and the beloved city; but fire came down from heaven and consumed them.

And the Devil who had deceived them was thrown into the lake of fire and brimstone where the beast and the false prophet were.

As we face the future, then, let us face it with assurance of final victory, though in the full knowledge that the future is a future of increasing conflict. The gospel will increasingly uncover every form of compromise and accommodation with evil, and will increasingly challenge every organ of power that corrupts the relations between men and usurps the authority which belongs to God alone;[67] until evil, finally stripped of all its disguises and because every alibi that it had has been exposed, will fight for itself in its own name and be destroyed. "Fire will come from heaven and destroy it."

The Opening of the Books *20:11–21:1, 5-8*

Then human history will be over. Earth and sky will flee away, and there will be no more sea.[68] It will be a new heaven and a new earth. And all the dead will come to judgment and they will be judged by what they had done.

This is how I saw it. I saw a great white throne, and Him who sat upon it. And I saw the dead, great and small, standing before the throne. They were judged by what was written in the books in which was recorded what they had done.[69] There was also another book, the book of Life,[70] and anyone whose name was not in it died the second death in the lake of fire.[71] Finally, Death and Hades also were

[66] Gog and Magog in Ezek. 38:2 are a prince and his land. In its Greek translation, the Septuagint turned these into names for nations.

[67] Col. 2:15.

[68] Isa. 51:9-10.

[69] John 5:22; II Cor. 5:10.

[70] Rev. 13:8.

[71] Gehenna was the valley of Hinnom in Jerusalem where the refuse of the city was burned. That which had perished (John 3:16) was here disposed of in the lake of fire.

thrown into the lake of fire and were consumed.[72]

Do you wonder what it means for men to be judged "by what they have done"? Remember the word of our Lord that he said: "When the Son of Man comes in His glory, and all the angels with Him, then He will sit on his glorious throne. Before Him will be gathered all the nations, and He will separate them one from another as a shepherd separates the sheep from the goats, and He will place the sheep at His right hand, but the goats at the left.[73] Then the King will say to those at His right hand, 'Come, O blessed of my Father, inherit the kingdom prepared for you from the foundation of the world; for I was hungry and you gave me food, I was thirsty and you gave me drink, I was a stranger and you welcomed me, I was naked and you clothed me, I was sick and you visited me, I was in prison and you came to me.' "

And He who sat upon the throne said: "Behold I make all things new." Also He said, "Write this, for these words are trustworthy and true." And He said to me,

> "It is done!
> I am the Alpha and the Omega,
> the beginning and the end.
> To the thirsty I will give water without price
> from the fountain of the water of life.
> He who conquers shall have this heritage
> and I will be his God and he shall be my son."

This is God's Word to you. It is the purpose and message of all that God showed to me to be imparted to you. What He began He will complete. What He has promised He will fulfill. The heritage is yours, inherit it.[74]

But as for the cowardly, the faithless, the polluted; as for murderers, fornicators, sorcerers, idolators, and all liars,[75] their lot shall be in the lake that burns with fire and brimstone, which is the second death.

[72] I Cor. 15:26.
[73] Matt. 25:31-36; Gal. 6:7-8.
[74] I Thess. 5:24; I Cor. 1:7-9.
[75] In Rev. 21:27, the phrase used is "anyone who makes a lie." This is the exact opposite of the Johannine phrase "doing the truth" (I John 1:6).

The Eternal City *21:2-4, 9–22:5*

Then came one of the seven angels who had the seven bowls full of the seven last plagues and spoke to me saying, "Come, I will show you the bride, the wife of the Lamb." And in the Spirit he carried me away to a great high mountain, and showed me the holy city Jerusalem coming down out of heaven from God, prepared as a bride adorned for her husband. And I heard a great voice from the throne saying:

"Behold, the dwelling[76] of God is with men.[77]
He will dwell with them and they shall be His people,
and God Himself will be with them;
He will wipe away every tear from their eyes,
and death shall be no more,
neither shall there be mourning, nor crying, nor pain anymore,
for the former things have passed away."

Let me describe to you the eternal city, the city of God's building, the city of man's inheritance.[78]

It was an open city. The city lay four-square, each side being twelve thousand furlongs in length. Also it had three gates on each side, which were never closed. All could come and enter except those who would not come. But, the walls of the city were twice twelve cubits high, and no one could climb over them.

It was a city of glory. Its radiance was that of a most rare jewel, like a jasper, clear as crystal. The walls too were built of jasper, while the city itself was of pure gold, clear as glass. The foundations of the wall were adorned with precious stones: jasper, sapphire, agate, emerald, onyx, carnelian, chrysolite, beryl, topaz, chrysoprase,

[76] The words "dwell" and "dwelling" used here literally mean "tabernacle," the word used also in John 1:14. This Greek word suggests by its sound the Hebrew word "*shekinah,*" which was the term used for God's presence in the tabernacle. At the close of the second section (11:19), the presence of God is represented by the ark in the temple. It was Jewish belief that when Jerusalem was destroyed Jeremiah hid the ark and that it would be restored when the Messiah came.

[77] John 1:14.

[78] Heb. 11:10.

jacinth, amethyst; and its twelve gates were twelve pearls, each gate a single pearl. Also, the street of the city was pure gold, transparent as glass.

It was the city of the saints. On its twelve gates were the names of the twelve tribes of the sons of Israel—there were three gates on each of the four sides—and on the twelve foundation stones[79] of the wall were inscribed the twelve names of the twelve apostles of the Lamb.[80] There were angels at each gate so that nothing unclean was there, nor could enter there. There was no one who practiced abomination or falsehood: but only those who were written in the Lamb's book of Life.

It was a city for the nations. There flowed from the throne of God and of the Lamb, through the middle of the city, the river of the water of life: and on both sides of it grew the tree of life with its twelve kinds of fruit, yielding its fruit each month.[81] And the leaves of the tree were for the healing of the nations. So did the nations walk in the light of the city, and the kings of the earth bring into it their glory. They brought into it the glory and honor of all the peoples of the earth.

It was the city of God. There was no temple there, for the Lord God, the Almighty, and the Lamb were its temple. Neither had the city need of sun or moon to shine upon it, for the glory of God was its light and its lamp was the Lamb.[82] There was no more anything accursed, but the throne of God and of the Lamb was in it, and His servants worshiped and served Him. They saw Him face to face and His name was on their foreheads.[83] They did not need light of lamp or sun, for the Lord God was their light, and they reigned with Him forever.

[79] In the ancient world a foundation stone was a witness to a claim, and not purely a memorial.

[80] Eph. 2:20; Ezek. 48:31.

[81] Cf. Gen. 3:22.

[82] John 1:4; 8:12.

[83] I John 3:2.

Seven Last Words

A Word of Reassurance

The angel said to me, "These words are trustworthy and true. And the Lord, the God of the spirits of the prophets, has sent His angel to show His servants what must soon take place.

And behold I am coming soon,
blessed is he who keeps the words of the
prophecy of this book."

A Word of Confirmation

I John am he who heard and saw these things. And when I heard and saw them, I fell down to worship at the feet of the angel who showed them to me; but he said to me, "You must not do that! I am a fellow servant with you and your brethren the prophets, and with those who keep the words of this book. Worship God."

A Word of Warning

And he said to me, "Do not seal up the words of the prophecy of this book, for the time is near—so near that there is hardly time even to repent.

Let the evildoer still do evil,
and the filthy still be filthy,
and the righteous still do right,
and the holy still be holy!

Behold, I am coming soon, bringing my recompense, to repay every one for what he has done. I am the Alpha and the Omega, the first and the last, the beginning and the end."

A Word of Promise

"Blessed are those who wash their robes, that they may have the right to the tree of life and that they may enter the city by the gates. Outside are the dogs and sorcerers and fornicators and murderers and idolators, and every one who loves and practices falsehood.

"I Jesus have sent my angel to you with this testimony for the churches. I am the root and the offspring of David, the bright morning star."

A Word of Invitation 17.

The Spirit and the Bride say, "Come."
And let him who hears say, "Come."
And let him who is thirsty come,
let him who desires take the water of
life without price.

The time indeed is short, but there is grace waiting to welcome all.

A Word of Admonition 18-19

I warn every one who hears the words of the prophecy of this book: if any one adds to them, God will add to him the plagues described in this book, and if any one takes away from the words of the book of this prophecy, God will take away his share in the tree of life and in the holy city.

A Word of Benediction 20-21

He who testifies to these things says,
"Surely I am coming soon."
Amen. Come, Lord Jesus!
The grace of the Lord Jesus be with all. Amen.

PLAN OF CONTENTS

John has delivered his message, but that message is not yet fully understood when it has simply been read. It has also a meaning which is conveyed only as its form is seen. The design and pattern of the book of Revelation are themselves part of what the book is about. Its message is also in the form in which that message is articulated.

Preliminary

The opening verses of the book explain themselves. They constitute a preliminary part which sets out what the book is about and what its nature is.

1:1-2, Title
1:3, Address
1:4-6, Greeting
1:7-9, Preface
1:10, 11, 19, Contents

Then follow the visions. Each vision is a unit, and each is meaningfully related to the others. This relationship is one of sequence as well as of repetition. Not only is each vision related to those which precede and follow it, but it is also related to the visions that belong to its own series in the developing movement of the whole book. This movement is spiral, not linear, in form.

It must also be remembered that John's symbolism is not pictorial. The symbols are not representations. They are ideas alive with color, sound, and form. So the task of exegesis becomes the task of tracing the several connections between these ideas, knowing that it is not always a logical connection which must be looked for. Often the connection is simply one of recall.

The Three Sections

Section One

Following the preliminary verses in the book, there is its first main part, which is a covering letter that John sends along with his message. This covering letter is addressed to the churches. It is addressed to them by their Lord.

The letter opens with a vision of the Lord, He who is the Bridegroom of His Church, and the vision is followed by what the Bridegroom has to say to His bride. He calls her to love and fidelity, and warns her against entanglement with false lovers. (The complement to the vision of the Bridegroom at the beginning of the book is the vision of the bride with which the book comes to its conclusion.)

1:12-18, The Opening Vision
2:1–3:22, The Letters to the Churches
- I-IV. The four churches tempted to compromise: Ephesus, Smyrna, Pergamum, Thyatira
- V. Sardis
- VI. Philadelphia
- VII. Laodicea

But judgment and renewal within the house of God are never an isolated experience. Judgment and mercy belong to the working of God in the world as a whole. It is the world that God is seeking to redeem. The first transition in the book of Revelation, therefore, is a transition from the theme of "the Lord and His Church" to the theme of "the Lord and His world."

This theme comes to its obvious climax in 11:15-19 with the declaration, "The kingdom of the world has become the kingdom of our Lord and of his Christ." The section following in chapter 12 is a further development of John's thought in which is described the concrete effect of the rule of God as that rule contends with the powers as John knew them in his own day.

Section Two

John opens his message concerning the coming of the Kingdom with another Christophany. The letters to the churches began with a vision of the Lord amidst the lamps; this section begins with a vision of the Lamb amidst the throne. It is a vision which speaks of the eternal realities. Here, in this vision, the hymn of redemption is already heard, and the revealing of the sons of God is already sure. The Lamb has redeemed a people unto Himself, and the book of Life with their names written on it is already in God's hand. But the book is not yet open. Heaven's joy is the joy of certainty, but it is also a joy in anticipation. Fulfillment comes only as the seals of time are broken.

This fulfillment is the inner meaning of the judgments of God, for all His judgments are also a call of repentance. They are, besides, the means by which the Remnant is gathered. The "gathering of the Remnant" is one of the themes of Scripture in its treatment of history. As each age comes to its harvest, not only is it overtaken by judgment, but that judgment also discloses who are the sons of God. It is this disclosure which mediates God's call to the world to repent. The "sons of God" suffer with and for the world, and in so suffering stand revealed: those who repent because of them bear witness about them that "by their stripes we are healed."

The book of Life is sealed with seven seals, and as each seal is broken, events happen which constitute a gradual ripening of the time when the book can be opened. Then the seventh seal is broken, the book is opened, and the sons of God are revealed. But the revealing of the sons of God is not the end of the process of judgment. Judgment continues; the sons of God, who have been revealed, making clear to the rest that judgment is a call to repentance.

Again and again, in the course of human history, events take place which correspond to the happenings that John portrays. Indeed, the simple fact that the happenings in this book have been identified with event after event through the centuries is ample proof of the sureness with which he understood the principles that determine the divine governance of the world, and of the appositeness of the symbols which he employs. Every fulfillment of the cycle of events which John describes marks a further stage in the coming of God's Kingdom, a further stage in which the results of sin become clearer, God's plea for repentance becomes more urgent, His power in human affairs becomes more evident, and His Church becomes more visible.

The Kingdom of God is something which has come, with stages of its fulfillment in the past; it is something which is coming, with signs of its fulfillment in the present; it is something which is to come, with the promise of its fulfillment in the future. In his vision of the throne in heaven, John describes the certainties whose foundation is the accomplished victory of the Lamb; in his portrayal of the course of God's judgment, he describes the process by which God's will is realized in the present; and then he turns, as this section comes to its climax, to the future, seeking to show what the final consummation will be. The end-event will be when "the kingdom of the world has become the kingdom of our Lord and of his Christ."

But this end-event is not all future; it is also present experience, for just as the Church shares in the sufferings of the world, it also shares in the sovereignty of the Christ. To the martyr church is given, again and again, that experience of victory which is an anticipation and an installment of that final rule of its Lord.

4:1–5:14, The Throne in Heaven
6:1–8:1, Judgment and Mercy
  I-IV. The four horsemen—the loss of peace
  V. Earthquake—the loss of stability
  VI. The sealed multitude
  VII. The unsealed scroll

8:2-5, The Altar in Heaven
8:6–11:19, The Wages of Sin and the Gift of the Kingdom
  I-IV. The four trumpets—the loss of subsistence
  V. Woes—the loss of faith
  VI. The gospel of redemption
  VII. The Kingdom comes

Section Three

Now takes place the next transition in John's writing. It is a transition from that situation in which men face both the judgment and mercy of God into a situation in which God is seen in active war with evil itself. John opens this section again with a Christophany, and then moves forward into a description of evil under the symbol of four monsters. But soon, and by an almost unnoticed shift of perspective, the evil with which God and His people are contending is portrayed in contemporary terms. Idolatry and adultery become questions of life and death, and faithfulness to the faith becomes the all absorbing concern.

God strives with the powers and overthrows them; they strive with God and come to their condemnation. The harvest of human history is reaped, the great city in which men became adulterous and idolatrous is destroyed and, amidst the lamentations of men at the passing away of so much that they held dear, there comes down from heaven the eternal city into which has been gathered the honor and riches of the nations. Faith leaps across the chasms of time and sees the end-event as immediate and proximate.

12:1-17, God's Purpose in Travail
13:1–14:20, Christus Imperator
I-IV. The four monsters—the rebellion of evil
V. The mark of the beast and of the Lamb
VI. The nature of judgment
VII. The close of an age

15:1-8, The Song of Salvation
16:1–19:4, Christus Victor
I-IV. The four plagues—the beginning of the end
V. The last issue
VI. Judgment executed
VII. The great city is no more

19:5-16, The Great Hallelujah
19:17–22:21, Christus Pantokrator
I-IV. The four powers—the end of their misrule
V. The final encounter
VI. The last judgment
VII. The eternal city

The book of Revelation is thus seen to consist of six movements. There is one movement in Section One, two movements in Section Two, and three movements in Section Three:

1. The Bridegroom and His bride
2. The Lamb and His people
3. The Lord and His world
4. Christus Imperator
5. Christus Victor
6. Christus Pantokrator

Each movement begins with a Christophany and proceeds through seven events. The basic materials which compose these events are also in units of seven—seven seals, seven trumpets, seven bowls, seven blessings, seven symbols of evil, seven pictures of the Church—but these primary units of seven are simply the raw material which John uses. They do not determine the basic pattern of his arrangement.

They are blended within his over-all design. Sometimes he groups together for massive effect those elements which belong to the same unit of seven, as in the case of the seven seals, trumpets, and bowls; whereas in the case of the seven benedictions, or the seven symbols of evil or of the Church, he distributes them throughout the book, producing thereby the effect of repetition or symmetry.

What, then, are the principles on which the design of the whole is constructed? The answer seems to be that the principles are to be found in the two realms within which the writing of the book of Revelation moves: the realm of history and the realm of liturgy.

THE WEEKLY SEQUENCE[1]

The basic unit of time sequence is the week, and John uses the week as his key to the unfolding of history. The week begins with Sunday, the day on which creation began. On this day light was created. The first vision of each of the six movements in the book of Revelation is thus set out as a Christophany. Christ is the light of the world.

Visions on Creation Sunday

1. Christ amidst the lamps
2. The Lamb amidst the throne
3. The Lord's people in supplication
4. The dragon against the child
5. The song of Moses and of the Lamb
6. The Bridegroom of the Church

All these visions are radiant with light. The first is illumined by the seven-branched lamp of the temple, the second is set amidst the glory of the throne in heaven, the third is seen in the glow of the charcoal on the altar, the fourth is joined to the vision of the woman in light, the fifth is heard across the fire of the crystal sea, the sixth is bright with the beauty of the bride as she receives her Bridegroom.

Following each Christophany are visions which set forward the story of man's life as it is lived amidst the temptations of the world: the lure of earth to compromise one's faith, the call of God to repentance and surrender. The events which these visions portray happen

[1] See Chart of the Historical-Liturgical Pattern of the Apocalypse, p. 115, for clarification of the apocalyptic pattern in the weekly sequence.

from Monday to Thursday, and there is a fourfold symbolism employed to tell their story.

The visions on Creation Sunday tell of events in heaven, the visions on the weekdays tell of events on earth. Four is the numeral symbol of earth.

Visions on the four weekdays

1. The four churches tempted to compromise
2. The four horsemen revealing sin's nature
3. The four trumpets calling to repentance
4. The four monsters rebelling against God
5. The four plagues executing judgment
6. The four powers finally destroyed

The primary units of the material which John uses here are in groups of seven, but these groups of seven are divided into 4 and 3—the four being massed together as shown above, and the three being woven into the general movement separately.

Following the weekday visions come the visions on Friday. These have the cross for their motif. The events they portray happen on Calvary. They are events concerning the temporary success of sin, the choice between life and death, the encounter between God and evil.

Visions on Friday

1. Sardis: dying but called to life
2. Martyrs: their cry and its response
3. Eagle: the vulture to the corpse
4. Branded: the mark of the beast and of the Lamb
5. Armageddon: the last issue
6. Gog and Magog: the final encounter

The Friday visions contain the heart of John's message to the churches. In these visions, his readers are, as it were, brought to the foot of the cross, there to see the meaning of their predicament and there to find encouragement for their faithfulness.

The Saturday visions are Sabbath visions. The Sabbath is, for the Christian, a day of promise. He looks forward to the Sabbath rest which is prepared for God's people when God's work shall have been completed, and when their tribulation and pilgrimage shall be over.

The Sabbath visions are, therefore, visions of events that are pointed to that future. They are concerned with the proclamation of redemption and the calling of the redeemed; they are also concerned with the declaration of judgment and its execution.

Visions on Saturday

1. Philadelphia—summoned to its apostleship
2. The host of the redeemed
3. The gospel of redemption
4. The nature of judgment
5. The judgment of Rome
6. The last judgment

"My Father worketh and I work," were the words of Jesus when challenged about the way in which He observed the Sabbath. John's conception of the Sabbath is controlled by this teaching. The Sabbath points to a work unfulfilled, it points to a Sabbath yet to come. As the writer to the Hebrews expresses it, "there remains a sabbath rest for the people of God."[2]

The guarantee of this "rest" is the victory of Easter day. John begins each movement with a Christophany on Creation Sunday and ends with a vision of "consummation" on Easter Sunday. That is the octave which is symbolic and basic to the movement of human history.

Visions on Easter Sunday

1. Laodicea: the Lord knocks at the door
2. The unsealed scroll: the sons of God are revealed
3. The last trumpet: the Kingdom comes
4. The harvest reaped: the close of an age
5. Lamentation: the great city is destroyed
6. The eternal city

The Festal Year[3]

John fulfills his design to set his visions within the perspective of history not only by using the weekly sequence as the symbol of his-

[2] Heb. 4:8.

[3] See Chart of the Historical-Liturgical Pattern of the Apocalypse, p. 115, for clarification of the apocalyptic pattern in the festal year.

torical development, but also by using the movement of the festal year. The weekly sequence carries the story from creation to consummation, the yearly sequence commemorates the great deeds of God which are at the heart of that story.

The Jewish festal year represented a continuous movement of the history of Israel from the celebration of its deliverance from Egypt up to the fulfillment of its destiny according to God's promise to Abraham. God had said to Abraham, "I will bless you, . . . so that you will be a blessing. . . . and by you all the families of the earth will bless themselves."[4]

1. *Passover*: The festive year began with the feast of the Passover. Before the feast itself was a period of preparation, at least a month, in which roads and bridges were repaired for the benefit of pilgrims. Also, on the day before the Passover, a search was made in each house to discover and throw out any leaven that happened to be left. This search was made with lit candles. Then, on the day of the Passover itself, was held the Passover meal.

The letters of John to the seven churches are concerned with this period of preparation. The churches must be got ready for the feast. The Lord is now searching out with lamps the leaven in their midst. Soon He will come and knock at the door. "If any man open" He says, "I will come in and sup with him and he with Me." He will come as both guest and host, He who is also the Passover lamb.

2. *Pentecost*: The period from the Passover to Pentecost, seven weeks afterward, was one season. The chief events of the season were related to the birth of spring and the gathering of first fruits from the fields. The spring of Israel began with their deliverance from Egypt, which act of God Israel celebrated by the sacrifice of the paschal lamb. Then came Pentecost, which was a thanksgiving festival for the harvest of first fruits. On this day was also celebrated the giving of the Law on Mount Sinai.

The next section of the book of Revelation opens with the vision of the Paschal Lamb but, as the story proceeds, it is not the Lamb that is slain but His followers. It is their blood which, as in the Passover rite, is poured at the base of the altar. But Passover ends with Pentecost. Moses brought the tablets of the Law, Jesus breaks the

[4] Gen. 12:2-3.

seals of the scroll of Life; and when the seals are broken the sons of God are revealed. They are the first fruits of the new age.

3. *New Year*: The people of Israel had a strong and stormy history. They drank the cup of bitterness to its dregs in their exile in Babylon. But they came back, and under Ezra and Nehemiah a new day dawned for them. Ezra read to them the Law of God and they rededicated themselves to Him. The festival of New Year celebrated this new day on the new-moon day of the seventh month. Trumpets sounded on this day in Jerusalem all day long. It was also a memorial of that day when, under Joshua, their fathers took possession of the land of their inheritance, when at the blowing of trumpets the walls of Jericho fell.

The message of the book of Revelation too moves from Pentecost to New Year. The prayer "How long" is heard again, the prayer of the people in exile. But soon the trumpets are sounding, the open scroll is read, Law and prophecy bear witness, and the Kingdom comes. "Awake, O sleeper, and arise from the dead, and Christ shall give you light."[5]

4. *Day of Atonement*: New Year ushered in a period of fasting, on the tenth day of which came the day of Atonement. Israel never forgot that in spite of their dedication to the Law, they had broken it again and again. At Mount Sinai itself, they had worshiped the golden calf, and Moses had to make atonement for their sin. Thus the day of Atonement became the fitting sequel to the feast of the New Year. It also stood between New Year and the feast of Tabernacles. Tabernacles celebrated the close of the harvest season, but before the joy of harvest must come the time of repentance and atonement. The harvest will also be the harvest of tares which is gathered and burned.

So, the final section of John's visions opens with the vision of Him who came to atone. The dragon is out to destroy Him. But though the period when wheat and tares grow together seems long, and those who bear the mark of the beast seem to rejoice over the sorrows of those who bear the mark of the Lamb, the harvest certainly comes. Then the wheat is garnered and the tares burned. Also, at the end

[5] Eph. 5:14.

of the harvest season the grapes are gathered and trodden in the wine press.

5. *Tabernacles:* This feast was the feast of the end of harvest. It announced the great certainty of the future, when Israel shall have completed its journey through the wilderness and the nations of the world would be its harvest fruit unto the Lord. But the feast was celebrated in temporary booths where the people dwelt, for that was still their present situation, as it was their situation on their journey through the wilderness. The Hallel sung at the feast was concerned with the salvation yet to come. "Oh work then now salvation, Jehovah" was what they sang.

"On that day," wrote the Prophet Zechariah, referring to the feast of Tabernacles, "the pots in the house of the Lord shall be as the bowls before the altar; . . . so that all who sacrifice may come and take them and boil the flesh of the sacrifice in them."[6] These bowls dominate the events which, at this point of his message, John portrays. The Hallel is heard—the song of Moses and of the Lamb—and then the bowls are emptied over the earth. The last sacrifice is the burning of evil.

6. *Dedication*: So the pilgrimage comes to its end. The wilderness and the exile are left behind. There is a final conflict. And then it is the New Day. When Judas Maccabeus rededicated the altar after setting his people free, and restored the worship of the Lord in the temple, it did seem that the New Day had dawned. Israel celebrated this day as the feast of Lights. They celebrated it on the day (December 25) when the sun after its long winter sojourn began its return journey in the heavens.

John closes his book, too, with the dawn of the New Day. The great hallelujah is heard as the nations are gathered into Zion. The final battle is fought and victory decisively won. The last judgment is over and the eternal city is established.

This Jewish festal year running from Passover to Dedication is fulfilled in the Christian story. At the Dedication, the old temple was restored for worship, at Christmas the new temple was set in the midst of men. God had become flesh. The chief rite in the celebration of the Dedication festival was the lighting of the sevenfold lamp; the opening

[6] Zech. 14:20-21.

vision in John's message is the Christ as He stands in the midst of His Church. The feast of Dedication closed the Jewish festal year; Christmas begins the festal year for the Christian Church.

The Daily Liturgy [7]

The design in John's writing reflects not only the structure of history as symbolized by the weekly sequence and the succession of the festal year; it reflects also the form of the liturgy. The book of Revelation is a service of praise on the Lord's Day.

It is in the book of Revelation that for the first time in Christian literature the term "Lord's Day" occurs. It was the day of the Lord's resurrection. But the practice of celebrating the Lord's resurrection every week rather than once a year seems to have been the way chosen by the early Christian community to confess their faith in Jesus Christ as Lord. There is evidence in two inscriptions from Ephesus and Kabbala and in an Oxyrhynchus papyrus of about A.D. 100 that a certain day of the week was observed during this time as "emperor's day." The weekly festival of the Church on the first day of the week was its silent protest against the imperial claim. In setting his visions within the context of the liturgy, John is bearing witness to the central significance of the worship of the Church.

The daily liturgy in the temple began with various activities designed to prepare for the service. Then, when everything was ready, the priest presiding directed one of the other priests to ascend a "pinnacle" and report the rising of the sun. Soon would be heard the cry "The morning shineth"; then the lamb would be brought and tied ready to be sacrificed. Also, the elders would give the order for the temple gates to be opened, whereupon priests would enter into the Holy Place to clean and trim the great seven-flamed lamp.

> Through an open door into heaven, John comes to attend the service. The lamps are burning and the lamb is ready for the sacrifice.

The opening of the gates was the signal for the slaying of the lamb. When the lamb was slain, its blood was caught up in a golden bowl,

[7] See Chart of the Historical-Liturgical Pattern of the Apocalypse, p. 115, for clarification of the apocalyptic pattern in the daily liturgy.

sprinkled on the altar, and then poured at the altar's base. Then followed all the details completing the sacrifice.

The sacrifice completed, the incensing priest and those assisting him approached the altar of burnt offering. Burning coal from the altar was placed in a golden bowl, incense was put into a golden censer, and the priests proceeded into the Holy Place. Here on the golden altar, the coal was spread and the priest stood ready to offer incense. The signal was given that the time of incense had come, whereupon the people fell down before the Lord spreading their hands in silent prayer. For a half hour silence was observed, while the smoke of incense rose unto the Lord.

> "I stand at the door and knock"—the Lamb is amidst the throne —the service begins. Soon, the blood of the martyrs is being poured at the base of the altar. At the close, when all the seals are broken, there is silence in heaven for a half hour. On the altar in heaven, the prayers of the saints are offered; incense and coal are brought there from the altar of burnt offering on earth.

Then the trumpets were blown, the meat of the sacrifice was thrown into the fire, and as the sacrifice was burning the Levites sang the psalms.

> The incense offering in heaven too is followed by the blowing of trumpets. But that which is slain and burned is not the followers of the Lamb but of the beast. As this judgment takes place, the song of deliverance is sung, the temple is filled with the smoke of incense, the bowls of wrath are poured out.

The libation took place along with the singing of the psalms, and then when the sacrifice had been completely consumed by fire, the psalmody rose to a great crescendo.

> So it is also in the heavenly service. The song of deliverance is followed by the great hallelujah. With that, the service is over, God and man are reconciled; and through the day, with all its daily duties, God and man will dwell together.

"Behold, the dwelling of God is with men. He will dwell with them, and they shall be his people."[8]

[8] Rev. 21:3.

Plan of Contents

History and liturgy belong together. Human life is supported by the deeds of God, from the deeds of God it gets its direction and destiny. These deeds of God determine also the content of man's worship. Man offers to God in worship what he has already received from God through grace. In that worship is man's essential participation with God in all that God is doing. History provides the stuff of liturgy, liturgy lifts history into the realm of doxology. "Herein is the patience and endurance of the saints."

Chart of the Historical-Liturgical Pattern of the Apocalypse

THE CYCLE OF TIME

THE DAILY LITURGY AND THE FESTAL YEAR

	SUNDAY	MONDAY—THURSDAY	FRIDAY	SATURDAY	SUNDAY	
DEDICATION *Lamps Dressed*	Christ amidst the lamps *(the opening vision)*	The temptation to compromise *(the four churches)*	Called to life *(Sardis)*	Summoned to apostleship *(Philadelphia)*	Invited to the feast *(Laodicea)*	PASSOVER *The Lamb Is Slain*
PASSOVER *Blood Offering*	The Lamb amidst the throne *(the throne in heaven)*	The ravages of of sin *(the four horsemen)*	Calamities on the earth *(the cry of the martyrs)*	The host of the redeemed *(the sealed multitude)*	The sons of God revealed *(the unsealed scroll)*	PENTECOST *Half-Hour Silence*
PENTECOST *Incense Offering*	The Church's supplication *(the altar in heaven)*	The call to repentance *(the four trumpets)*	Woes upon the soul *(the shout of the eagle)*	The gospel of redemption *(the open scroll and the two witnesses)*	The Kingdom comes *(the last trumpet)*	NEW YEAR *The Trumpet Is Blown*
ATONEMENT *Burnt Offering*	God's purpose in travail *(the dragon against the child)*	The rebellion of evil *(the four monsters)*	Choice between life and death *(the mark of the beast and of the Lamb)*	The nature of judgment *(the four harvest cries)*	The close of an age *(the harvest reaped)*	ATONEMENT *The Victim Burns*
TABERNACLES *Drink Offering*	Bowls of wrath and the song of deliverance *(the prolepsis of faith)*	The beginning of the end *(the four plagues)*	The last issue *(Armageddon)*	Sentence is executed *(the judgment of Rome)*	Consumed by fire *(lamentation)*	TABERNACLES *The Victim Consumed*
DEDICATION *Levitical Psalmody*	The Bridegroom arrives *(the great hallelujah)*	Christus Pantokrator *(the four powers)*	The final encounter *(Gog and Magog)*	The last judgment *(the opening of the books)*	The grand consummation *(the eternal city)*	DEDICATION *Amen*
	CREATION	WORLD	CALVARY	SABBATH	EASTER	

THE DAILY LITURGY AND THE FESTAL YEAR

THE PROCESS OF HISTORY

THEOLOGICAL MEDITATIONS

The Subject of Revelation (1:1-2)
The Nature of Time (1:3)
The Situation of the Christian (1:4-6)
The Being of God (1:7-9)
The Necessity of Decision (1:10, 11, 19)
The Object of Faith (1:12-18)
The Verdict of Love (2:1–3:22)
The Ruler of the Universe (4:1–5:14)
The Dissolution of History (6:1-8)
The Wrath of the Lamb (6:9-17)
The Tribulation of Life (7:1-17)
The Redemption of Sons (8:1)
The Hope of the Gospel (8:2-5)
The Fall of Nature (8:6-12)
The Wages of Sin (8:13–9:21)
The Mystery of Mercy (10:1–11:11)
The Reversal of Man (11:12-19)
The Motherhood of Grace (12:1-17)
The Manifoldness of Evil (13:1-10; 17:1-18)

TO THE READER

Each meditation in this section is based on a passage from the book of Revelation. The Scripture references will be found in the italicized headings which appear at the top of each page. To locate related material in other sections of *As Seeing the Invisible,* the reader should consult the Scripture and Subject Indexes (pp. 187 ff.).

Title *1:1-2*

THE SUBJECT OF REVELATION

"Surely the Lord God does nothing,
without revealing his secret
to his servants the prophets."[1]

God is the source of all revelation. What John receives and communicates is from God. It comes to John with the testimony of Jesus to it, the only testimony that can guarantee it to be a revelation from God. "No one has ever seen God; the only Son, who is in the bosom of the Father, he has made him known."[2]

It is God who is made known. For He is not only the source but also the subject of all revelation. All revelation is from God and is about God. So that while John seems to speak of events in the future, in reality he is declaring the Word of God, that which reveals God's thought and nature. The characteristic of prophecy is insight more than foresight, the ability to see the meaning of things in the light of eternity.

The book of Revelation is not a book about "times or seasons";[3] it is rather a book about God in whose hands times and seasons are. Indeed, we must not expect it to be a revelation of times and seasons, for no one knows them, "not even the angels of heaven, nor the Son, but the Father only."[4]

When John, therefore, says that the revelation is concerning "the things which must soon take place," he intends the emphasis to fall on the word "must." He is speaking of a necessity which is the result of God being God and sin being sin. It is the same kind of necessity as that to which Jesus referred when He said, "The Son of man must be delivered into the hands of sinful men, and be crucified, and on the third day rise."[5]

These things which are necessary will also happen quickly. The word "quickly" carries both the meanings which John intends. For John is speaking not only about the time that must elapse before these

[1] Amos 3:7.
[2] John 1:18.
[3] Acts 1:7.
[4] Matt. 24:36.
[5] Luke 24:7.

things happen (i.e., soon), but he is speaking also of the time that these things will take when they do happen. They will happen "in the twinkling of an eye,"[6] they will arrive "like a thief in the night."[7]

And it is because these things will happen quickly that they also present themselves as about to happen shortly. They have the quality of always being there, near at hand, impending. It is this quality of being impending which causes that foreshortening of prophetic vision that makes the prophets declare God's visitation to be always near. What is certain is also imminent.

> "The time is fulfilled, and the kingdom of God is at hand; repent, and believe in the gospel."[8]

[6] I Cor. 15:52.
[7] I Thess. 5:2; Rev. 16:15; cf. Mark 13:35.
[8] Mark 1:15.

The Nature of Time

> ". . . it is full time now for you to wake from sleep. For salvation is nearer to us now than when we first believed; the night is far gone, the day is at hand."[1]

Time is not simple duration which men can fill with happenings according to their will. Time is fraught with God's plans and purposes, and comes to men with a quality of challenge in it. Each next moment comes to a man not as a blank for him to fill with a thought or word or deed as he thinks best. It comes, rather, laden with God's will for him, which he disobeys at his peril.

The Bible, whenever it speaks of time, speaks of it in this way. It sees time as something which comes from God and is instinct with God. So that when John says, "The time is near," he means God is near.

This is always true, and faith knows it to be so; but at certain times this nearness of God is discernible even to sight. God flashes into view with judgment and mercy. Such a time is time's fulfillment.

The phrase in the New Testament which is translated "the end of the world" is more correctly translated "the coming to head of an age."[2] It includes the idea of this present material world as constituting an age to be followed by another age, another state of being which is spiritual; but the primary reference of the phrase is rather to those periods of history when an age reaches its consummation and comes under judgment—its good to be gathered in and its evil to be destroyed.[3]

"So it will be at the close of the age. The angels will come out and separate the evil from the righteous, and throw them into the furnace of fire, . . . Then the righteous will shine like the sun in the kingdom of their Father."[4]

At a period of history when one such consummation was seen to be near, John wrote his book. To all who have faith to know, it is a

[1] Rom. 13:11.
[2] Matt. 24:3.
[3] Matt. 13:39; Rev. 14:14-20.
[4] Matt. 13:49, 43.

book whose message is relevant for any time, while there are times when its relevance becomes obvious even to one's naked eyes.

We live in such a time today.

> "Blessed . . . are those who hear the word of God and keep it."[5]

[5] Luke 11:28.

The Situation of the Christian

> ". . . in Christ shall all be made alive. But each in his own order: Christ the first fruits, then at his coming those who belong to Christ. Then comes the end, when he delivers the kingdom to God the Father after destroying every rule and every authority and power."[1]

Jesus already reigns. He has been declared to be both Lord and Christ.[2] But this reign of Christ is only the portal of the Kingdom of God. The Kingdom, when the Father shall be all in all, is yet to come.[3] Hence it is that John changes the usual Jewish description of God as Him "who was and is and shall be"[4] into Him "who is and was and is to come." The future is already present tense. The Kingdom of the Father is already present in promise in the Kingdom of the Son.

But with Christ's kingship we have already entered into the end of times. Creation already awaits its deliverance.[5] The end has already begun. And it will reach completion because of the continual working of God's Spirit. The kingship of Christ is present fact, the Kingdom of God in its fullness is future event, the work of the Spirit is the continuous process that links these two together.

But why a process at all? Because, although the act of redemption is complete—He has freed us from our sins[6]—yet the power of sin is not destroyed. We are freed because sin is bound, but even in its captivity sin has the power to rebel; and this rebellion is a terrible thing. God's unfailing love, however—He loves us[6]—guards His children and sustains them.

This is the central situation—the rebellion of captive sin—which John describes in his book although, as he insists, the days of sin are numbered and the victory of God is certain. Grounded in such a certainty we have both grace and peace from God; and living by it we ascribe to God both glory and dominion.

[1] I Cor. 15:22-24.
[2] Acts 2:36.
[3] I Cor. 15:28.
[4] The Targum paraphrase of Exod. 3:14.
[5] Rom. 8:19.
[6] Rev. 1:5.

For we, who are Christ's people, not only have a Kingdom, but are a Kingdom, an organized society realizing the will of the divine King and proclaiming that will to the world. Even as Christ is God's faithful witness, we too must be; even as Christ was raised from the dead, we too shall be; that even as Christ is ruler of the kings of the earth, we too may be.[7] He is the first-born among many brethren.[8]

> "Write the vision;
> make it plain upon tablets,
> so he may run who reads it.
> For still the vision awaits its time;
> it hastens to the end—it will not lie.
> If it seem slow wait for it;
> it will surely come, it will not delay."[9]

[7] I Cor. 6:2.
[8] Rom. 8:29.
[9] Hab. 2:2-3.

THE BEING OF GOD

"Who is like the Lord our God,
  who is seated on high,
Who looks far down
  upon the heavens and the earth?"[1]

God has His seat on high, but He humbles Himself. He is transcendent; His immanence in the world is the expression of His humility. It is a humility that led Him even to take on human flesh.[2]

The transcendence of God is a description of His being, His immanence is an act of will. Thus, although God is immanent in the world and shares in its strife, we know already the issue of that strife, for He who is transcendent will transcend. To this strategic truth John calls the attention of his readers again and again.

In his Preface he does this in two ways. First of all, he speaks of God as "the Alpha and the Omega,"[3] which means not merely that God is the beginning and the ending, but rather that God is the all-comprehending entirety, whose nature and whose will control all events. And second, he speaks of God as "Almighty,"[4] He who, by Himself, is able to accomplish His will.

This word "Almighty," while it occurs eight times in the book of Revelation, occurs but once in the rest of the New Testament, and that in a quotation from the Old Testament.[5] It is a word that holds for John the same significance that the term "the Lord of hosts" held for the armies of Israel.[6] It was the guarantee of final victory.

This juxtaposition in thought, between a conflict that is not yet over and a victory that is already sure, is peculiar to the Bible. The opposition which the armies of Israel faced in the land of Canaan was incident to the fact that they had already entered into possession. The

[1] Ps. 113:5-6.
[2] Phil. 2:5-8.
[3] Rev. 1:8.
[4] Rev. 1:8; cf. Gen. 17:1; Exod. 6:3.
[5] II Cor. 6:18; Jer. 31:9.
[6] In the Septuagint the term "Lord of hosts" is rendered by a word which means "Almighty." It is the same word that is used here.

difficulties which the Christians were facing belonged to a time which was after the Kingdom of God had actually come.

There is an end-time, the time after the end has begun. The end began with Jesus, the Christ. "The lightning of his coming had been seen, now the thunder of his final triumph is to sound."[7] But before that, tribulation.[8] Tribulation is that dark hour before the dawn.

> "I have said this to you, that in me you may have peace. In the world you have tribulation; but be of good cheer, I have overcome the world."[9]

[7] A. T. Hanson.
[8] Acts 14:22.
[9] John 16:33; cf. II Thess. 3:5; Luke 21:19.

The Necessity of Decision

> "And Joshua said to all the people, '. . . choose this day whom you will serve, . . .' Then the people answered, '. . . we . . . will serve the Lord, for he is our God.' But Joshua said to the people, 'You cannot serve the Lord; for he is a holy God, . . . If you forsake the Lord and serve foreign gods, then he will turn and do you harm, and consume you, after having done you good.' "[1]

That which is real cannot be manipulated to suit our conveniences and our desires. It is intransigent and objective. It demands decision. We must either decide for it and obey its implications or decide against it and abide by the results. That God in Christ is the ultimate reality is the message of the book of Revelation, and its purpose is to call men to decision with respect to Him.

The choice of men is set between God and God's rival—God's rival being no mere description of man's sinfulness, but that to serve which is accounted sin. Jesus calls it mammon,[2] the things of this world (safety, security, wealth, power, position) which men seek to possess and which in their seeking they allow to possess them. The writer of the Fourth Gospel calls it the world,[3] that ordering of nature and of human affairs independent of the will of God. Paul calls it sin,[4] organized unrighteousness with servants in its pay. The book of Revelation calls it the red dragon,[5] the eternal enemy of God.

It is a real choice between two masters which man is bidden to make; so that John, in challenging men to make that decision, emphasizes, on the one hand, the glory and joy of discipleship to God, while, on the other hand, he insists on the reality and terror of judgment on those who reject Him.

John's treatment of the theme of God's judgment, however, is misunderstood if we do not remember that the agent of God's judgment as John sets Him forth is the Lamb that was slain. The judgments of God are judgments of grace; they spring from "the impossible

[1] Josh. 24:2, 15-20.
[2] Matt. 6:24; Luke 16:13.
[3] John 7:4; 16:33.
[4] Rom. 6:23.
[5] Rev. 12:3.

mercy of giving us the blessing of the light which we hate."[6] It is true that sometimes John seems to forget this quality of God's judgment, but we may not forget it.

Using this theme of judgment as the key to the book of Revelation, the book naturally divides into three parts:

Section I. Chapters 1–3: God judges the Church, which He will chasten and redeem.

Section II. Chapters 4–11: God judges the World, which He will afflict and reclaim.

Section III. Chapters 12–22: God judges the Devil, whom He will punish and destroy.

"O Lord, . . . in wrath remember mercy."[7]

[6] F. D. Maurice
[7] Hab. 3:2.

THE OBJECT OF FAITH

"For in him the whole fulness of deity dwells bodily, . . .[1]

The first word of the book of Revelation is the word "unveiling" (i.e., revelation), and the first object that is unveiled is He who is described as the Alpha and the Omega. Indeed, an unveiling of God, as the Beginning and the Ending and as from the Beginning to the Ending, is the main purpose of the whole book.

John's opening vision of the Son of Man is his exposition of this theme, for it is in and through Jesus Christ that God is unveiled. It is Jesus who is the central figure of Scripture, the Messiah of Jewish prophecy and apocalypse, the bearer and author of the Eschaton, the end-event. Hence the appropriateness of the Old Testament imagery in which John presents the picture of the ascended Lord.[2]

In apocalyptic language, the phrase "like a son of man"[3] means one who is more than man but whose true personality is discerned by faith. To the eye he seems to be a man only. It was the term that Jesus used most about Himself, and it is a term that is valid even now. For though Jesus is ascended Lord, His lordship is still apprehended by faith alone.

And those who thus apprehend Him remain unshaken "though the earth should change, though the mountains shake in the heart of the sea; though its water roar and foam, though the mountains tremble with its tumult."[4]

> Yet that scaffold sways the future, and, behind the dim unknown,
> Standeth God within the shadow, keeping watch above his own.[5]

There is a close connection between the messages which are delivered to the churches and the description of Jesus in this vision. The simple truth is that the message to the churches is Jesus Himself. What John is doing is to administer to his hearers the sacrament of the Word.

[1] Col. 2:9 (bodily—as one organic whole).
[2] Dan. 7:9-13; 10:5-6; Ezek. 43:2; Isa. 49:1-2.
[3] Dan. 7:13; cf. Acts 7:56.
[4] Ps. 46:2-3.
[5] James Russell Lowell, from "The Present Crisis."

Through his words he mediates to them the presence of the Word made flesh. That Word is the Word of God to them. To contemplate Him is to listen to Him also.

> "Be still and know that I am God.
> I am exalted among the nations,
> I am exalted in the earth!"[6]

[6] Ps. 46:10.

THE VERDICT OF LOVE

"For your Maker is your husband,
the Lord of hosts is his name;
and the Holy One of Israel is your Redeemer."[1]

The Genesis story of man's sin holds at its center God's cry of anguish over the sinner. "Adam! Adam! Where are you?"[2] This cry continues down the centuries bearing witness to God's unfaltering love to wayward men.

"How can I give you up, O Ephraim!
How can I hand you over, O Israel!"[3]

"Come now, let us reason together,
says the Lord:
though your sins are like scarlet,
they shall be as white as snow;
though they are red like crimson,
they shall become like wool."[4]

"O Jerusalem, Jerusalem, . . . How often would I have gathered your children together as a hen gathers her brood under her wings, and you would not!"[5]

This love of God even took human flesh that it might pour itself out on men the more,[6] and when men rejected it and crucified it, it neither bent nor broke but gave itself up in prayer of forgiveness for them.[7] Such love must win. It will.

It is this confidence in the triumph of God's love in Jesus Christ which is basic to the seven letters to the churches. They are "at once seven Epistles addressed to seven churches, and one Epistle addressed to the church; individual portraits of seven Christian communities, and one composite portrait of the whole; anticipations of the future of

[1] Isa. 54:5.
[2] Gen. 3:9 (adapted).
[3] Hos. 11:8.
[4] Isa. 1:18.
[5] Matt. 23:37.
[6] John 3:16.
[7] Luke 23:34.

each but also principles which must govern the fate of all."[8]

And the main cry of the letters is this, that the Church, afflicted as she is by "fightings within and fears without" should turn to her Bridegroom who is also her Maker and Redeemer, and give to Him again the love of her espousals.[9] The sound of that "knock"[10] with which the letters close declares the right of Him who knocks to enter. He knocks as rightful Lord and not in humble supplication. Yet, as John would have us remember, love waits outside in persistent patience until the door is opened from within.

It is a picture of judgment and of mercy—of judgment because love is inexorable and of mercy because love is kind.

> "And I will betroth you to me for ever; I will betroth you to me in righteousness and in justice, in steadfast love, and in mercy."[11]

[8] C. A. Scott, "Revelation," *The Century Bible,* Edinburgh: T. C. & E. C. Jack, n.d.,) p. 135.

[9] Jer. 2:2.

[10] Rev. 3:20.

[11] Hos. 2.19.

The Ruler of the Universe

"How beautiful upon the mountains
are the feet of him who brings good tidings,
who publishes peace, . . .
who says to Zion, 'Your God reigns.' "[1]

The good news of the book of Revelation is the certainty that God is King, that there is a throne in heaven, that the universe is not without a Ruler.[2] To one bound by earthly sight the forces of the world seem determinative of the final outcome of history: but he who has eyes to see and ears to hear can discern in the assurance of the heavenly hosts, as they sing their songs of praise, the certainty of the triumph of the purposes of God.[3]

It is not enough to be concerned with the problems of earth; one must also see those concerns from the point of view of heaven.[4] It is before God who is on the throne that the world must justify itself. All attempts to justify God before the world and from the world's point of view are not only misleading but blasphemous.[5]

The throne in heaven, however, is a throne within a temple, and not a palace: a temple in which not only the songs of praise are heard but also where the incense of prayer is raised. There the heavenly priesthood make intercession with the saints for the world,[6] and there the Lamb of God wields sway as an abiding sacrifice for His people.[7] The rule of the universe is is in the hands of creative power and redemptive love.

John's symbols of God's presence are the throne and the temple, and it is characteristic of John's thought that when describing God's relation to a sinful world he specially uses the temple symbol. It is from the temple that many of God's judgments proceed.[8] Even the throne of God is set within a rainbow, the rainbow proclaiming God's patience with the sons of men.[9] So does the cross become the sign of

[1] Isa. 52:7.
[2] Rev. 19:6.
[3] Ps. 46; Hab. 2:3.
[4] Rev. 4:1.
[5] Job 40:8.
[6] Rev. 5:8.
[7] Heb. 10:12.
[8] Rev. 11:19; 14:15-20; 15:6-8; 16:17-18.
[9] Gen. 9:13.

triumph, and the patient weakness of love the sign of its strength.

There is therefore no reason for weeping, for though the Church is beset with trials, He who began His good work will also finish it.[10] He who has redeemed His people will perfect their redemption. He who has written their names in the book of Life will open that book.

> ". . . that at the name of Jesus every knee should bow, . . . and every tongue confess that Jesus Christ is Lord."[11]

[10] Phil. 1:6.
[11] Phil. 2:10.

The Dissolution of History

"Every kingdom divided against itself is laid waste, and no city or house divided against itself will stand."[1]

Man is both the creature of earth and the child of God,"[2] but because he is God's child he refuses to be earth's creature also and he attempts to usurp equality with God.[3] The result is sin. Thus does the Bible explain the nature of sin, and shows how it corrupts man's creative energy.

Man builds his civilizations but is unable to resist the temptation to make these civilizations the expression of his own autonomous worth.[4] So every civilization ends in a Babel, a house divided against itself, autonomous man unable to support the ideal of human brotherhood.[5]

John opens his story of judgment with this picture of man against man, or rather of nation against nation: for it is in the complex life of a nation that it is most possible to disguise the limitations of man. A nation is able to claim autonomy with some plausibility—a claim, however, which inevitably results in one form or another of search for conquest and, therefore, war. And war is the precursor of famine, of pestilence, and of death.

Thus when John speaks of the second rider as being commissioned by God to shatter "the peace of the earth," he is giving expression to God's longing for the breakup of that façade of peace which civilizations wear over their inner tensions.

As civilization succeeds civilization, or as power passes from group to group, those who have eyes to see discern the real character of history because they discern the character of man. These have no more confidence in the historical process as such, but see it rather as a process of repentance—of man's gradual discovery, through many experiments, of his absolute dependence on God for worth as well as for security.[6]

Victory does not consist in the achievement of power but in being found worthy to wield it. To the Son belongs all authority, for He

[1] Matt. 12:25.
[2] Gen. 2:7.
[3] Gen. 3:5; 11:4.
[4] Mark 12:7.
[5] Gen. 4:8.
[6] Jer. 2:13.

has overcome. He has overcome the temptations of His sonship,[7] the lure of the power He wields. By this victory He controls the destinies of men until they learn from Him how they too may overcome.

> "Nevertheless do not rejoice in this, that the spirits are subject to you; but rejoice that your names are written in heaven."[8]

[7] Matt. 4:3; 11:27; 17:5.
[8] Luke 10:20.

The Wrath of the Lamb

> "As surely as I saw yesterday the blood of Naboth and the blood of his sons—says the Lord—I will requite you on this plot of ground."[1]

The story of God's judgment is a story that is as old as history.[2] God does punish sin, and yet how often the saints of God exclaim, "O Lord, how long shall I cry for help, and thou wilt not hear? Or cry to thee 'Violence!' and thou wilt not save?"[3] The mystery of God's judgment is not that it happens, but that so often it tarries so long. It is the mystery of the wrath of the Lamb, of an anger that is redemptive, of a vengeance that is patient.[4]

The cry of the martyrs for vengeance, as John represents it, may seem to us to be wrong: and yet it is a cry which must find an echo in the prayers of all God's people who are concerned with the vindication of right and the overthrow of wrong.[5] It is a false sense of values which prefers the avoidance of suffering to the punishment of evil. It is a coward's choice to cease to pray that evil be brought home to the evildoer lest behind the prayer there operate also the motive of personal revenge.

Besides, why may we not pray for judgment when we know that the Judge of all the earth will do right?[6] When we know that wrath is of the Lamb? Indeed, it is more than significant that John represents the sight of the face of the Lamb[7] as man's ultimate judgment and punishment.

In his poem on judgment entitled "Well," G. A. Studdert-Kennedy makes this point with uncommon force. A soldier has found the truth that meeting Jesus is his final destiny and this is what he says:

> I's got to follow that I's seen,
> Till this old carcass dies;
> For I daren't face in the land o' grace
> The sorrow o' those eyes.

[1] II Kings 9:26.
[2] Isa. 5:25.
[3] Hab. 1:2, 13; cf. 2:2-3.
[4] Rom. 12:19.
[5] Matt. 23:35; Luke 18:7, 8.
[6] Gen. 18:25.
[7] Rev. 6:16; cf. I Pet. 3:12.

There ain't no throne, and there ain't no books,
  It's 'Im you've got to see,
It's 'Im, just 'Im, that is the Judge
  Of blokes like you and me.
And, boys, I'd sooner frizzle up,
  I' the flames of a burnin' 'Ell,
Than stand and look into 'Is face,
  And 'ear 'Is voice say—"*Well?*"[8]

"And the Lord turned and looked at Peter, and Peter went out and wept bitterly."[9]

[8] *The Best of Studdert-Kennedy* (New York: Harper & Brothers, 1948), p. 160.
[9] Luke 22:61, 62 (adapted).

THE TRIBULATION OF LIFE

> "I have said this to you, that in me you may have peace. In the world you have tribulation; but be of good cheer, I have overcome the world."[1]

The verb that lies behind the noun "tribulation" means "to make into gruel." What is pictured is a process of grinding between an unyielding bottom and an oppressing top. When applied to the Christian life, this means that the Christian stands crushed between the unyielding demands of his totalitarian faith and the oppressive challenge of the world for compromise.

A Christian can therefore speak of life itself as "the great tribulation,"[2] using the specific experience of "persecution" as a symbol of it. When Jesus first used the phrase "the great tribulation," He used it of the destruction of Jerusalem.[3] To John the phrase signifies rather the great persecution of the Church which he sees to be imminent in his own time. But as John thinks of the multitude in heaven, the phrase broadens out in his mind and he talks of "the great persecution" in a way that is descriptive of life itself.[4]

What happens as a result of tribulation? The revealing of the sons of God![5] It is this which John seeks to describe in the story of the breaking of the seals and the opening of the book of Life. It is the uncovering of the sons of God for the world to see, the making actual in the flesh of God's purpose of sonship for men. There is a sealed book to be opened, there is a sealed multitude to be revealed. They that are sealed belong to him whose seal they bear.[6] He will be made manifest and, with Him, they also.

This destiny embraces all, Jews and Gentiles alike. As John pictures it, the redeemed in heaven are from every race and nation, of every tribe and tongue, and they bear palm branches in their hands. Zechariah had prophesied a day when the Gentiles, too, would carry palm branches as a sign of their deliverance, and partake in the feast of Tabernacles—the feast which commemorated the journey of the

[1] John 16:33.
[2] Rev. 7:14.
[3] Matt. 24:21.
[4] Cf. Acts 14:22.
[5] John 16:21; cf. Rom. 8:19.
[6] II Cor. 1:22; Ezek. 9:4.

Jews from Egypt to Canaan as well as celebrated the completion of the harvest season.[7]

> "And after you have suffered a little while, the God of all grace, who has called you to his eternal glory in Christ, will himself restore, establish, and strengthen you."[8]

[7] Zech. 14:16.
[8] I Pet. 5:10.

THE REDEMPTION OF SONS

> "You are the salt of the earth; . . . You are the light of the world."[1]

"I am the light of the world," said Jesus. "He who follows me will not walk in darkness, but will have the light of life."[2] This light, which is Christ, is the light that the Christian reflects. "To be light" is the calling with which he is called. We bear witness that He is the light. We may not evade, however, His bidding that we be light too.

Light illuminates. In it, the meaning and proportion of things become visible. It also makes clear one's direction of movement. By it one knows where one is going. John is describing the breaking of the seals of time. The meaning and direction of this process, he says, is the revealing of the sons of God. By this process also the proportion of things is determined. It is this future event that controls and illumines human history. Though it is in the future, yet it is the meaning of the whole. Man's story is lit up from in front. "We know that the whole creation has been groaning in travail together until now; and not only the creation, but we ourselves, who have the first fruits of the Spirit, groan inwardly as we wait for adoption as sons, the redemption of our bodies."[3]

The work of salt is to preserve from decay. Without it the world would rot as dead flesh. But let that flesh be seasoned with salt and it is made fit to be offered as sacrifice. Thus were all sacrifices salted which were made under the old covenant,[4] and thus will the sacrifice under the new covenant be salted too. "For every one will be salted with fire."[5]

The story of man is not a story of decay and dissolution. It is a story of God's covenant with man whereby God comes to man as man's possession, so that man may come to God with God, and be His.

A sealed scroll in the hand of the king contains the king's decree. When that scroll is taken, its seals broken, and its contents read out,

[1] Matt. 5:13-14.
[2] John 8:12.
[3] Rom. 8:22-23.
[4] Lev. 2:13.
[5] Mark 9:49.

then that decree has been promulgated. This is the symbol that John employs. The Son promulgates the decree of the Father. He makes the Father's will to happen.

> "Beloved, we are God's children now; it does not yet appear what we shall be, but we know that when he appears we shall be like him, for we shall see him as he is. And every one who thus hopes in him purifies himself as he is pure."[6]

[6] I John 3:2-3.

The Hope of the Gospel

> "Now when these things begin to take place, look up and raise your heads, because your redemption is drawing near."[1]

The reign of God becomes actual in history not only as men accept that reign, but also as God imposes that reign on human affairs. Whenever God's character becomes clearer, His demand for repentance is reinforced by judgment, and His Church becomes more visible as a separate and separated community; then we may say that there is a coming of the Kingdom of God.

The New Testament does speak of a coming of Christ in a final sense, to bring to a head the whole process of history,[2] but the majority of its references to His coming point rather to a repeatable event—a series of crises in an ongoing process.[3] Indeed, the word "parousia,"[4] which is translated "coming," a word that connotes the periodic visit of a king to the territories that belong to his empire. We are a colony of heaven and the King visits us too.[5] That this teaching of the New Testament has been so largely misunderstood is due to the fact that we have learned to use the phrase "the *second* coming of Christ" to designate His final coming in glory.

There have been many comings of God and there still will be, and one thing we may learn from the book of Revelation is how to discern them when they happen. For in this book we have a treatment of the essential nature of each of these processes—of the revelation of God's character, of the reinforcement of the demand for repentance with judgment, of the becoming-visible of the Church of Christ.

It is this becoming-visible of the Church as a separate and separated community that is emphasized here, a separateness that is realized through tribulation and is recognized in it. ". . . suffering produces endurance, and endurance produces character, and character produces

[1] Luke 21:28.

[2] Eph. 1:10; I Cor. 15:24; Heb. 9:28.

[3] Matt. 24:27, 44.

[4] I Thess. 2:19. (It was the practice when the emperor came to present him with a crown.)

[5] Phil. 3:20.

hope, and hope does not disappoint us. . . ."[6] To this separated community, living by its hope in its returning Lord, belongs the task of prayer as its primary function. It is a priesthood[7] mediating between God and the world. Also, by its prayer it partakes in God's effective rule, who uses that prayer to manifest His power.[8]

> "For it was fitting that he, for whom and by whom all things exist, in bringing many sons to glory, should make the pioneer of their salvation perfect through suffering."[9]

[6] Rom. 5:3-5.
[7] I Pet. 2:5.
[8] Jas. 5:16.
[9] Heb. 2:10.

The Fall of Nature

"It is written,
Man shall not live by bread alone,
but by every word that proceeds from the mouth of God."[1]

The first events which John describes after "the revealing of the sons of God" are a series of natural disasters. The Jews thought of nature as in a fallen condition.[2] It was not as God intended it to be, and yet it is what God intends as the home of fallen man. An imperfect world is the only kind of world in which sinful men can discover both themselves and God.

"Cursed is the ground because of you;
in toil you shall eat of it all the days of your life;
thorns and thistles it shall bring forth to you; . . .
In the sweat of your face
you shall eat bread."[3]

Where bread does not constitute a problem, the Word of God tends to become a luxury. Where nature offers no threat to man's sufficiency, the soul's dependence on God is rarely recognized.

How paradoxical to man's real situation is Jesus' advice when He says, ". . . do not be anxious about your life, what you shall eat or what you shall drink, nor about your body, what you shall put on. . . . But seek first his kingdom and his righteousness, and all these things shall be yours as well."[4]

And how apposite to man's real situation in the world is Habakkuk's faith when he says:

"Though the fig tree do not blossom,
nor fruit be on the vines,
the produce of the olive fail
and the fields yield no food,
the flock be cut off from the fold
and there be no herd in the stalls,

[1] Matt. 4:4.
[2] Rom. 7:20-25.
[3] Gen. 3:17-19.
[4] Matt. 6:25, 33.

K

yet I will rejoice in the Lord,
I will joy in the God of my salvation."[5]

It is characteristic of John's perception that he makes this real situation of man come alive as the result of the prayers of the saints. The disasters which happen, happen as the prayers of the saints on earth are mingled with the prayers in heaven and are then returned to earth as an instrument of God's rule.

> "Let not the wise man glory in his wisdom, let not the mighty man glory in his might, let not the rich man glory in his riches; but let him who glories glory in this, that he understands and knows me, that I am the Lord who practice kindness, justice, and righteousness in the earth; . . ."[6]

[5] Hab. 3:17-18.
[6] Jer. 9:23.

The Wages of Sin

"The wages of sin is death, but the free gift of God is eternal life in Christ Jesus our Lord."[1]

Sin pays wages. It is a taskmaster with servants in its pay. Much so-called modern knowledge has destroyed for us the objectivity and hence the horrible reality of sin. In terms of the theory of evolution we call sin "imperfection," and trust to "progress" to set it right. In terms of a new psychology we call sin a "disease," and trust the psychotherapist to heal it. In terms of our theories of education we call sin just "ignorance," and believe that enlightenment will cure it. In terms of sloppy sentiment we call sin mere "error," and hope that "maturity" will change it. What we have lost is a view of sin in terms of God![2]

Sin is God's rival bidding for the service of man,[3] and although under God's control, is His rival nevertheless. John probably believed in the literal existence of demons such as he describes,[4] and we may not; but John's pictures are true in that they teach us to think of sin apart from our sinning.[5]

And yet, by itself, no perception of sin as it truly is leads to repentance. It may induce terror and remorse, but nothing more.[6] Salvation comes only as the result of a vision of God. John makes this extraordinarily clear. Sin is like some python which hypnotizes us into impotence: and from which there is no escape except under a stronger influence. It is not the fear of sin but the love of God which sets men free.[7]

> And can it be that I should gain
> An interest in the Saviour's blood?
> Died He for me, who caused His pain?
> For me, who Him to death pursued?
> Amazing love! how can it be
> That Thou, my Lord, shouldst die for me?

[1] Rom. 6:23.
[2] Ps. 51:4; Isa. 6:5.
[3] Matt. 6:24.
[4] Rev. 9:1-21.
[5] John 1:29.
[6] Rev. 9:6, 20.
[7] Rom. 5:8; Rev. 1:5.

Long my imprisoned spirit lay,
Fast bound in sin and nature's night;
Thine eye diffused a quickening ray,
I woke, the dungeon flamed with light:
My chains fell off, my heart was free,
I rose, went forth, and followed Thee.[8]

"If you love me, you will keep my commandments. And I will pray the Father, and he will give you another Counselor, to be with you for ever."[9]

[8] Charles Wesley.
[9] John 14:15-16.

The Mystery of Mercy

> ". . . the Lord said in his heart, . . . neither will I ever again destroy every living creature as I have done. . . . When the bow is in the clouds, I will look upon it and remember the everlasting covenant between God and every living creature. . . ."[1]

One of the recurrent themes of the Bible is the punishment that inevitably overtakes sin; but this theme is never treated in isolation. It is always placed alongside the thought of the persistent mercy of God, whose judgment tarries, and with whom forgiveness is always present.[2] This character of God is constantly felt to be inexplicable. Why does He care for man so much?[3]

This mystery of divine restraint haunts the pages of the Old Testament until it becomes an open secret[4] with God's action in Christ. In Christ the mystery is revealed: not that God's mercy ceases to be a mystery to sinful man, but that it is a mystery which is now known —a mystery on which man can build his life with assurance, living henceforth by faith in the faithfulness of God.[5]

It is this conception of the nature of divine grace as affording perspective to the fact of divine judgment which John sets forth in his symbols of the rainbow and the *open* scroll. Thus, when the angel announces that the "mystery of God is finished," then we are prepared for God's action as it issues in judgment which tarries no longer.

The other symbol which John uses is that of Jerusalem and the two witnesses. Jerusalem is God's own city;[6] the world, too, is equally God's. Man is God's by right. The Church's task is simply to call men to repentance and to fidelity.[7] Apart from this, all programs to reform life piecemeal are but, at their best, efforts to be kind; and, at their worst, attempts to make spiritual adultery tolerable.[8]

[1] Gen. 8:21; 9:16; Isa. 1:18-20.
[2] Exod. 20:5 (cf. Ezek. 18:4); Hab. 1:2-3.
[3] Ps. 8:4.
[4] The word "mystery" in the New Testament means "open secret."
[5] Rom. 1:17.
[6] Rev. 11:8.
[7] II Cor. 5:20.
[8] Matt. 9:16.

The witnesses whom John describes exercise their primary function. They speak to the world about justice and self-control, and future judgment.[9] It is appropriate that they are clothed in sackcloth for "no one ought to speak of hell without a very tender heart."[10]

> "How the faithful city
> has become a harlot,
> She that was full of justice!
> Righteousness lodged in her, . . .
> but now murderers.
> Therefore the Lord says,
> I will turn my hand against you
> and will smelt away your dross as with lye
> and remove all your alloy."[11]

[9] Cf. Acts 24:25.
[10] Dwight L. Moody.
[11] Isa. 1:21, 24, 25.

THE REVERSAL OF MAN

> "Jesus of Nazareth, . . . you crucified and killed by the hands of lawless men. But God raised him up, . . ."[1]

The cross of Christ is the center of history. There both human sin and divine love touched bottom, so that we who live this side of Calvary know what the last word of history will be. It will be a word of forgiveness for man—Father, forgive them for they know not what they do—a forgiveness that will issue in the deed of Easter day. The end of history will be the word of Easter morning writ large over every act of man, reversing every deed of man's disobedience and establishing the wavering fidelity of the men of faith.

> We live by faith in God, the Father of our Lord Jesus Christ.
> Above all and in all and through all is the Holy Will, the Creative Purpose, of the Most High. The world is His and He made it. The confusions of history are in the grasp of His manifold Wisdom. He overrules and works through the purposes of men, bringing to nought their stubborn and rebellious lust for power but building their fidelity into the structure of His Reign upon earth.[2]

No one can foretell, however, the exact shape that the end-events of history will take: but one thing we know, that there is an end and that God is its architect.[3]

"Howbeit we speak wisdom among those who are mature: only it is not the wisdom of this world, nor of the rulers of this world who are coming to nought. It is the mysterious Wisdom of God that we discuss, that hidden wisdom which God decreed from all eternity for our glory.

What no eye has ever seen,
What no ear has ever heard,
What never entered the mind of man,
God has prepared all that for those who love him."[4]

[1] Acts 2:22-24.
[2] *The World Mission of the Church*, report of IMC World Meeting, Tambaram, 1938 (London: International Missionary Council, 1939), p. 14.
[3] Heb. 11:10.
[4] I Cor. 2:6-9, RV.

And this we also know that even as God's deed on Easter day provides the pattern of what God finally will do, even so it carries with it the assurance of what God repeatedly does after each Calvary.[5] There is no one who has shared the pain who has not also shared the power.[6] There is no time when the Church has discharged its task of witness when it did not also receive God's witness to it that it is from God.[7]

> "Now to him who is able to strengthen you according to . . . the revelation of the mystery which was kept secret for long ages but is now disclosed, . . . according to the command of the eternal God—to the only wise God be glory for evermore through Jesus Christ! Amen."[8]

[5] Luke 20:16-17; cf. I Cor. 1:27-28; I Pet. 2:4.
[6] Phil. 3:10.
[7] Heb. 2:4.
[8] Rom. 16:25-27.

The Motherhood of Grace

> "On those who have accepted him, however, he has conferred the right of being children of God, that is, on those who believe in his name, who owe this birth of theirs to God. . . . For we have all been receiving grace after grace from his fullness."[1]

God's grace is our mother.[2] She gave birth to us as children of God's household: and we remain children, receiving from her grace upon grace. This is our authority to say that we are the children of God.[3]

Grace is free and makes free.[4] She brought us forth and mothers us without any of our deserving, so that there is no need to make payment of any kind for what we have received,[5] except that gratitude prompts responsive love.[6] And the purpose of God's grace in bringing us forth is this, that "we should be holy and blameless before him . . . according to the purpose of his will, to the praise of his glorious grace. . . ."[7] On earth, we live by and for this purpose; grace is our abode; while in heaven grace remains the city to which we are bound and to which we really belong, our parent city: "the Jerusalem above, [which] is free, and she is our mother."[8]

> Begotten by Thy grace,
> Thy love we humbly prove,
> And seek to live before Thy face
> With hope unconquerable;
> The city of our God,
> The light of our long way,
> She bids us to our sure abode—
> The joy of eternal day.[9]

John represents this aspect of God's motherhood under the symbol of light, emphasizing it as the source and origin of all God's children,

[1] John 1:12, 13, 16 (adapted).
[2] The Greek word in John 1:13 which is translated "born" can also mean "brought forth" as applied to the mother of a child.
[3] Luke 15:21-22.
[4] Rom. 3:24.
[5] Rom. 11:6.
[6] I John 4:19.
[7] Eph. 1:4-6.
[8] Gal. 4:26.
[9] Charles Wesley.

Jesus being the first born. And even as Jesus grew into fullness of stature through suffering, so, says John, must all God's children grow.[10] "For he looked forward to the city which has foundations, whose builder and maker is God."[11]

> "Now the word of the Lord came to me, saying, 'Before I formed you in the womb I knew you, and before you were born I consecrated you.' "[12]

[10] Rev. 12:17.
[11] Heb. 11:10.
[12] Jer. 1:5.

The Manifoldness of Evil

"In that day the Lord with his hard and great and strong sword will punish Leviathan the fleeing serpent, Leviathan the twisting serpent, and he will slay the dragon that is in the sea."[1]

Whenever the Bible speaks of evil, it speaks of it as an incursion into human life from outside the universe.[2] The universe—that which God has made—is "order," but outside this "order" lies "disorder." It is outside, not in any spatial sense, but rather in the sense that it is outside human understanding and human reckoning.[3] The sovereignty of God includes His sovereignty over evil too;[4] but, as far as man is concerned, God's sovereignty over evil, while it supplies man with a ground for ultimate hope,[5] does not bring evil itself within man's calculation and control.[6]

It is this perception of the mystery of evil which underlies the biblical contention that evil can be mastered by God's Word alone,[7] and that it will be destroyed ultimately simply by God's fiat[8] when in the grand consummation the universe itself as such will pass away.[9]

This mystery of evil manifests itself in various forms, seeking to seduce men's loyalty: and men have to contend against each form as it appears, fully realizing that no victory of theirs over sin is final. Satan may fall as lightning, but it is not his last fall; so that it is nothing to rejoice over and to be content with.[10]

Slavery is abolished, but the exploitation of man by man remains and takes many forms. Woman is liberated from the position of being a chattel, but man's respect for woman has still to maintain itself against the assaults of suggestive fashions, sophisticated social conventions, and the influence of cheap literature. Man wages eternal war against the forms of evil, while evil itself remains and takes on other forms.

[1] Isa. 27:1.
[2] Matt. 4:3; 13:28.
[3] II Thess. 2:7.
[4] Luke 11:20-22.
[5] Rom. 8:28.
[6] I Pet. 5:8-10.
[7] I John 2:14; cf. John 15:3; Eph. 6:17.
[8] Rev. 19:13; 20:10; Heb. 4:12.
[9] Rev. 21:4.
[10] Luke 10:17-20.

Evil is man's predicament,[11] a predicament from which God alone can deliver him.[12]

> "And lead us not into temptation, but deliver us from evil: For thine is the kingdom, and the power, and the glory, for ever. Amen."[13]

[11] I John 5:19; cf. Matt. 4:19.
[12] Rom. 7:24-25.
[13] Matt. 6:13, AV.

The Assurance of Heaven

"... this is the victory that overcomes the world, our faith."[1]

One of the significant convictions of the book of Revelation is in its teaching that the war on earth is between the Lamb and the beast, and not between the Lamb and the dragon. The war with the dragon is over,[2] having been fought in the heavenly places where the dragon has been conquered. And, as John pictures it, when the hour strikes, the dragon yields unresistingly to its doom. "And he [the angel] seized the dragon, . . . and bound him for a thousand years, and threw him into the pit, and shut it and sealed it over him, . . . And when the thousand years are ended, . . . the devil . . . was thrown into the lake of fire and brimstone."[3]

In heaven there are no doubts about the ultimate issue of the conflict, no delusions about the falseness of the enemy, no wistful listening to his blandishments. Things are seen and known as they are. "So we do not lose heart. Though our outer nature is wasting away, our inner nature is being renewed every day. For this slight momentary affliction is preparing for us an eternal weight of glory beyond all comparison, because we look not to the things that are seen but to the things that are unseen; for the things that are seen are transient, but the things that are unseen are eternal."[4]

What the Christian needs is vision: the eyes of faith which can see the invisible.[5] And what John seeks to do in his book is to open our eyes that we may see, and seeing, take courage.

> "When the servant of the man of God rose early in the morning and went out, behold, an army with horses and chariots was round about the city. And the servant said, 'Alas, my master! What shall we do?' He said, 'Fear not, for those who are with us are more than those who are with them.' Then Elisha prayed, and

[1] I John 5:4.
[2] Rev. 12:9; John 12:31.
[3] Rev. 20:2, 3, 7, 10.
[4] II Cor. 4:16-18.
[5] Heb. 11:27; cf. Prov. 29:18.

said, 'O Lord, I pray thee, open his eyes that he may see.' So the Lord opened the eyes of the young man, and he saw; and behold, the mountain was full of horses and chariots of fire round about Elisha."[6]

[6] II Kings 6:15-17.

THE CERTAINTY OF JUDGMENT

"His winnowing fork is in his hand, to clear his threshing floor, and to gather the wheat into his granary, but the chaff he will burn with unquenchable fire."[1]

There is a long interval between sowing and reaping, and during this interval wheat and tares must grow together.[2] Any attempt prematurely to root out the tares can result in destroying some wheat. God's harvest, however, is timely and thorough. No grain of wheat, not even the smallest, will be lost when God gathers in those who are His own.

This long period of waiting after sowing is, then, the surest sign that there will be a harvesting. Nothing is for nought. All will be harvested whether it be seed sown by the Son of Man or by the Devil.[3]

In the parable of the prodigal son,[4] the turn of the story is the famine in the far country. That young boy left his father's home, many years elapsed before his wealth was exhausted, but soon enough he had to reap the harvest of his act of independence. The famine, however, turned him homeward. It was a harvest unto repentance.

In the parable of the wicked husbandman,[5] there is the clear suggestion that delay is not the result of forgetfulness. The householder kept on sending his servants to his tenants. Year after year they were asked to return to their landlord the share of fruit which was his. Then came the final reminder and the last chance. It was their last chance, too. They killed the son. When the householder himself arrived, he arrived with judgment. The harvest the tenants reaped was the harvest of retribution.

In the parable of the rich fool[6] there is a double harvest which is the theme of the story. The rich man reaped his fields while he himself was reaped of God. But the two harvests contradicted one another. It is not possible to serve God and mammon.[7] To attempt to do so ends

[1] Luke 3:17.
[2] Matt. 13:30.
[3] Matt. 13:37, 39.
[4] Luke 15:11-32.
[5] Matt. 21:33-43.
[6] Luke 12:16-21.
[7] Matt. 6:24.

in disillusion. The ultimate result of such a life is the harvest of remorse.

In the parable of the buried treasure,[8] the man who found the treasure found it as a result of his work—he plowed—but the treasure itself was not the result of his plowing. It was given. When he found the treasure, he went and sold everything he had and bought that field in which the treasure was. It is when all of life is invested in possessing what God has provided that life finds its final fulfillment. So comes the harvest of rest.

> ". . . I press on to make it my own, because Christ Jesus has made me his own."[9]

[8] Matt. 13:44.
[9] Phil. 3:12.

The Fulfillment of the End

"For the Son of man came to seek and to save the lost."[1]

The lost is found. There is fulfillment at the end. God's plan for the fullness of time, to unite all things in Christ, is accomplished.[2]

There shall never be one lost good! What was, shall live as before;
The evil is null, is naught, is silence implying sound;
What was good shall be good, with, for evil, so much good more;
On the earth the broken arcs; in the heaven a perfect round.
All we have willed or hoped or dreamed of good shall exist;
Not its semblance, but itself; no beauty, nor good, nor power
Whose voice has gone forth, but each survives for the melodist
When eternity affirms the conception of an hour.[3]

A recurring phrase of John's in his letters to the churches is "he that overcometh."[4] John's reference is not to those who win the race, but to those who complete it. "To overcome" does not mean to beat one's fellow runners, but to defeat the obstacles of the race itself. To arrive at the finish, that is victory.[5] It is this victory that is assured. It is this victory that God will win.

How does this happen? It happens because the Lord of the harvest is also the seed that is sown. He said to His disciples that the grain of wheat must fall into the earth and die if it is to bear fruit.[6]

"When he makes himself an offering for sin,
he shall see his offspring."[7]

It happens also because the Judge of the world is its Savior, too. The blood He sheds is His own blood, it is on Himself that His judgment falls. The grapes He tramples in the wine press of His wrath are those whom He has redeemed and for whom He died.

And finally, it happens because the end is already promised in the

[1] Luke 19:10.
[2] Eph. 1:10.
[3] Robert Browning, from "Abt Vogler."
[4] Rev. 2:7, 11, 26; 3:5, 12, 21; 21:7, AV.
[5] II Tim. 4:7.
[6] John 12:24.
[7] Isa. 53:10.

beginning. "For in him all things were created, . . . all things were created through him and for him, . . . and in him all things hold together."[8]

Is it then well, well for all, irrespective? No, for only the lost will be found. That which has perished has to be destroyed, they who have died can only be buried or burned.

> "For God so loved the world that he gave his only Son, that whoever believes in him should not perish but have eternal life."[9]

[8] Col. 1:16-17.
[9] John 3:16.

THE PERSISTENCE OF PITY

> "Though I removed them far off among the nations, and though I scattered them among the countries, yet I have been a sanctuary to them for a while in the countries where they have gone."[1]

It is God who has punished, but it is also God who has been a sanctuary to them in their punishment. Indeed, there had been no punishment were it not true that God was with them.

Israel had said, "I will go after my lovers"; but God's love will not let her go. "I will hedge up her way with thorns," He says, and 'I will build a wall against her, so that she cannot find her paths."[2]

The psalmist gives beautiful testimony to this character of God:

"He does not deal with us according to our sins,
nor requite us according to our iniquities.

. . . .

As a father pities his children
so the Lord pities those who fear him.
For he knows our frame;
he remembers that we are dust."[3]

Punishment and redemption belong together, they are the results of the same love. And if, as in this vision, John speaks of a punishment which does not reform, but destroys, it is yet a true insight by which he brings together the pouring of the bowls of wrath and the singing of the song of deliverance. Even today there is sung this song at Easter time, the Song of Moses and of the Lamb.

Come ye faithful, raise the strain
Of triumphant gladness;
God hath brought his Israel
Into joy from sadness,
Loosed from Pharoah's bitter yoke
Jacob's sons and daughters;

[1] Ezek. 11:16.
[2] Hos. 2:5-6.
[3] Ps. 103:10-14.

Led them with unmoistened foot
Through the Red Sea waters.[4]

In John's vision, the world is in its sunset, but over it sweeps this song with rapturous joy. Even at the end, when God puts an end to all rebelliousness, the meaning of His action is deliverance and not destruction, and His reason is not anger but pity.

> "You pity the plant, for which you did not labor, nor did you make it grow, which came into being in a night, and perished in a night. And should not I pity Nineveh . . . ?"[5]

[4] John of Damascus.
[5] Jonah 4:10-11.

The Death of the Soul

"Truly, I say to you, they have their reward."[1]

Men find what they seek, and every false search is rewarded by its consequences. Evil is punished by being allowed to bear its fruit until, like a cumulative poison, it destroys at the last those that live by it.

> A soul made weak by its pathetic want
> Of just the first apprenticeship to sin,
> Which thenceforth makes the sinning soul secure
> From all foes save itself, soul's trueliest foe,—
> Since egg turned snake needs fear no serpentry.[2]

The soul lives in the presence of God. It lives by His presence. Its life is its image-relation to God. But sin seeks to set up a cancerous growth within the soul, a growth persistently destroyed by God's forgiving and judging grace, and yet a growth which can finally withstand His mercy. "I will . . . put a new spirit within them; . . . that they may walk in my statutes and keep my ordinances. . . . But as for those whose heart goes after their detestable things, . . . I will requite their deeds upon their own heads. . . ."[3]

One of the astonishing features of the book of Revelation is the way in which it sets forth evil as a parody of the good. Evil is a trinity: the dragon, the first beast, and the second beast. There is a death and resurrection in the common belief about Nero. The followers of the beast bear a mark even as do the followers of the Lamb. The mystery of iniquity is as much a mystery as the mystery of redemption.

There is a profound truth which underlies this way of picturing evil. It is the truth that man is made for worship and that, if he will not worship God, he will worship some other power that claims his absolute obedience. Indeed, John goes further and suggests that man's nature is attuned to the worship of a trinity and the adoration of an incarnation. But, let this worship be of a substitute god, and men will

[1] Matt. 6:5.
[2] Robert Browning, from "The Ring and the Book," XII.
[3] Ezek. 11:19-21.

find that it destroys the image in which they have been created, and, destroying that image, destroys them also.

> No mean trick
> He left untried, and truly well-nigh wormed
> All traces of God's finger out of him:
> Then died, grown old.[4]

Is it any wonder that Jesus spoke of the dead burying the dead![5]

> "See to it that no one makes a prey of you by philosophy and empty deceit, according to human tradition, according to the elemental spirits of the universe, and not according to Christ."[6]

[4] Robert Browning, "Paracelsus."
[5] Luke 9:60.
[6] Col. 2:8.

The Suicide of Wrong

> "He disarmed the principalities and powers and made a public example of them, triumphing over them in him."[1]

Every principality and power is under God. If they are armed, they are armed by Him and for His purpose. "You would have no power over me," said Jesus to Pilate, "unless it had been given you from above."[2] However, when the ax vaunts itself over him who hews with it, or the saw magnifies itself against him who wields it, then must God disarm such a boaster.[3]

> "Though Babylon should mount up to heaven,
> and though she should fortify her strong height,
> yet destroyers would come from me upon her,
> says the Lord. . . ."[4]

To every principality and power is made known the manifold wisdom of God;[5] where that wisdom is contested, the powers engage one another in strife and destroy themselves. The soul which finally wins its release from God dies; every principality or power which acts independently of God also is destroyed. Within God's wisdom and plan they have their place; outside that wisdom they commit suicide.

In the ancient story of Babel,[6] man was rescued from the result of his own pretension by God who interfered; at the end this interference will be removed and man's pretension will be allowed to work out its own consequences. When that happens, evil, for the last time, will overreach itself and come to its destruction. Evil overreached itself when it crucified Jesus Christ, and God's Easter-event proclaimed the promise that that is how evil will be destroyed. In Christ, God triumphed over principalities and powers; in Christ, that triumph at last will be made secure and complete.

In the meanwhile, faith keeps watch over those who live by hope rooted in the resurrection of Jesus Christ, and sets their eyes toward that salvation which is ready to be revealed in the last time.[7]

[1] Col. 2:15.
[2] John 19:11.
[3] Isa. 10:15.
[4] Jer. 51:53.
[5] Eph. 3:10.
[6] Gen. 11:1-9.
[7] I Pet. 1:3-5.

"I tell you my friends, do not fear those who kill the body, and after that have no more that they can do. But I will warn you whom to fear: fear him who, after he has killed, has power to cast into hell—there to destroy both soul and body—yes, I tell you, fear him!"[8]

[8] Luke 12:4-5; Matt. 10:28 (adapted).

The Punishment of Power

"Come, let us build ourselves a city, and a tower with its top in the heavens, . . ."[1]

The history of human civilization must be studied in the shadow of Babel. It is the story of man's grasp for power foiled by his finitude. It is also the story of man's attempt to wield power as if it belonged to him, and belonged to him by right.

Power belongs to God, and only he has the right to wield it who receives it from God. They, however, who achieve it by force ultimately pay the cost of it, their unity being "confounded" and destroyed by division among themselves. The co-operative use of grasped power is not a long-term possibility. Power is the harlot, the great seducer of men. But, in the end, it also betrays them.

It is here that we see the significance of John's insight, in that he represents Rome as being finally destroyed by the beast itself. "And the ten horns that you saw, they and the beast will hate the harlot; they will make her desolate and naked, and devour her flesh and burn her up with fire, . . ."[2] In John's time Babylon was Rome, but Babylon never dies.

Jeremiah had prophesied the destruction of the original Babylon.[3] H. V. Morton gives us this picture of her destruction.

> . . . I saw on every side sandy mounds lying in the sunlight of mid-day: some were large enough to be called hills, others were low ridges, and still more were only uneasy risings and fallings of the earth. But for miles around, . . . the earth was blasted and unhappy with the memory of Babylon. So this was the city whose Hanging Gardens were among the Seven Wonders of the World. Four-horsed chariots could pass each other on its walls; on one altar alone a thousand talents' worth of incense was burned every year. . . . And as we wandered over the lonely mounds, silent except for the hum of the wild bee and the hornet, I thought how literally . . . [the] prophecy of the fall of Babylon had been fulfilled. It is, indeed, overthrown as God overthrew Sodom and Gomorrah. . . . The "broad walls" of Babylon have been "utterly broken" as Jeremiah

[1] Gen. 11:4.
[2] Rev. 17:16.
[3] Jer. 50:23-40.

prophesied; her gates have been "burned with fire;" the city has indeed become "an astonishment" and "an hissing without an inhabitant. . . ." What word better describes this awful desolation: "and Babylon shall become heaps."[4]

> "A ruin, ruin, ruin I will make it; there shall not be even a trace of it until he comes whose right it is; and to him I will give it."[5]

[4] H. V. Morton, *Through Lands of the Bible* (New York: Dodd, Mead, & Company, 1938), pp. 72-73, 77.

[5] Ezek. 21:27.

THE WASTE OF WEALTH

"Every valley shall be filled,
and every mountain and hill shall be brought low,
and the crooked shall be made straight,
and the rough ways shall be made smooth;
and all flesh shall see the salvation of God."[1]

In John's account of the lamentation that arose on the fall of Rome, there is poignant reference to all that Rome stood for in art, human civilization, and culture. But all man's wealth comes to nought. However, when John describes the new Jerusalem, he describes it in grander terms and fills it with all the wonder of Rome and more.[2] God overturns, but He also restores.

Said Paul: "It was his loving design, centered in Christ, to give history its fulfilment by resuming everything in him."[3] Somehow God does it over again, and includes within His doing all that God's loving purpose will not see lost of man's achieving.

In the "Magnificat" is the declaration of what certainly must happen, that they who bow to God's strong arm will also be raised by that arm to their full inheritance.[4] It is hard to comfort those who laugh. It is difficult to feed those who are full. It is impossible for those who think that they already have their inheritance to leave it behind and walk along the narrow path and through the narrow gate.[5] But, it is with these impossibilities and difficulties that God deals. Men may lament for a while, but joy comes in the morning.[6]

"He has shown strength with his arm,
he has scattered the proud in the imagination of their hearts,
he has put down the mighty from their thrones,
and exalted those of low degree;
he has filled the hungry with good things,
and the rich he has sent empty away.

[1] Luke 3:5-6.
[2] Rev. 21:1–22:21.
[3] Eph. 1:10, Ronald A. Knox.
[4] Luke 1:46-55; cf. Matt. 5:4, 6.
[5] Luke 6:24; 18:23; Matt. 7:14.
[6] Ps. 30:5.

He has helped his servant Israel,
in remembrance of his mercy, . . ."

"My soul magnifies the Lord,
and my spirit rejoices in God my Savior,
for he has regarded the low estate of his handmaiden.
For behold, henceforth all generations will call me blessed;
for he who is mighty has done great things for me,
and holy is his name."[7]

[7] Luke 1:51-55, 46-49.

THE CONSOLATION OF THE SAINTS

"Comfort, comfort my people,
 says your God.
Speak tenderly to Jerusalem,
 and cry to her
that her warfare is ended,
 that her iniquity is pardoned,
that she has received from the Lord's hand
 double for all her sins."[1]

The hand of judgment and discipline has been not only on Babylon but also on Jerusalem. In truth, God's act of judgment upon the nations fell most heavily on His own people set within the nations and scattered among them. They always had proof, by the discipline they endured, that they were sons of the Father and were being treated as sons. "For what son is there whom his father does not discipline?"[2]

Wheat and tares are together everywhere. The sons of the Kingdom and the sons of the Evil One live together until the close of the age.[3]

No wonder that the harvest, when it comes, is accompanied both by a great lamentation and by a great hallelujah. Indeed, the hallelujah is the more spontaneous, for the denouement is, to the saints, the more unexpected. They never dreamed that their God was so near even through all those hours of darkness, so near that when the darkness lifted they saw Him. He did not have to arrive; He had always been there. He had come when it was still dark.[4]

There is in the New Testament a constant emphasis on the imminence of the coming of the Lord and, therefore, the necessity on the part of the Church to watch for the coming.[5] This imminence is grounded in the certainty of His constant presence. As, when lightning flashes, the darkness lifts, and that which is there is seen to be there; so will it be at the coming of the Lord.[6] The constancy of His presence, the imminence of His coming, and the certainty that He will come—

[1] Isa. 40:1-2.
[2] Heb. 12:7.
[3] Matt. 13:38.
[4] Mark 6:48.
[5] Mark 13:32-37.
[6] Matt. 24:27.

all belong together as one truth, and are known together as truth in the experience of the saints.

> "I will not leave you desolate; I will come to you. Yet a little while, and the world will see me no more, but you will see me; because I live, you will live also. In that day you will know that I am in my Father, and you in me, and I in you."[7]

[7] John 14:18-20.

The Foretaste of the Kingdom

> ". . . sealed with the promised Holy Spirit, which is the guarantee of our inheritance until we acquire possession of it. . . ."[1]

The crisis of event, an ongoing experience, a foretaste of the future —that is always the pattern of the biblical doctrine of last things.

Thus God's Judgment is a series of repeated crises in history—"I will overturn, overturn, . . . until he come whose right it is."[2] It is an ongoing process—"And this is the judgment, that the light has come into the world, and men loved darkness rather than light, . . ."[3] It is also a future event—"Then I saw a great white throne . . . and the dead were judged . . . by what they had done."[4]

The Resurrection, too, is a crisis that belongs to this life—". . . the hour is coming, and now is, when the dead will hear the voice of the Son of God, and those who hear will live."[5] At the same time, it is a continuous experience—". . . that as Christ was raised from the dead . . . we too might walk in newness of life."[6] It is also a future event—". . . the hour is coming when all who are in the tombs will hear his voice and come forth, those who have done good, to the resurrection of life, and those who have done evil, to the resurrection of judgment."[7]

So has also the Kingdom of God a threefold reference. It is fact— ". . . the kingdom of God has come near."[8] It is process—"For the kingdom of God is . . . righteousness and peace and joy in the Holy Spirit."[9] It is hope—"Thy kingdom come."[10]

Thus when John speaks of the millennial reign of Christ on earth, we shall understand him best if we think of it also according to this pattern. It is the continuous experience of the Church in its resurrection life; it is a series of crises which will overtake history, in which the rule of God in the affairs of men will be openly recognized and conscientiously obeyed; it is the guarantee of Christ's complete vic-

[1] Eph. 1:13-14.
[2] Ezek. 21:27, AV.
[3] John 3:19.
[4] Rev. 20:11, 12.
[5] John 5:25.
[6] Rom. 6:4.
[7] John 5:28-29.
[8] Luke 10:11.
[9] Rom. 14:17.
[10] Matt. 6:10.

tory at the end. That John speaks of the millennium simply as one event is due to the fact that he is expressing his conviction of the certainty of the millennial experience in terms of the category of immediacy. This way of speaking is a common characteristic of prophecy.

". . . believe in God, believe also in me."[11]

[11] John 14:1.

The Close of the Ages

"Thy kingdom come,
Thy will be done,
On earth as it is in heaven."[1]

But will it come on earth? Yes. We notice how John sets out Christ's millennial reign as a weekday vision depicting an earthly event. And yet, there will be no time on earth when we can cease to pray, "Thy Kingdom come." That prayer will cease only when the Kingdom has finally come, when both heaven and earth as we know them now shall have passed away, and when all things have become new.[2]

The dragon, death, and Hades belong to the structure of history as we know it now, and they constitute the dividing line between earth and heaven. Only for Jesus is it true that that line does not exist, for He has conquered all three.[3] He is risen. But the day will come when all the dead shall rise, and when these three shall have been finally destroyed.[4] Then will heaven and earth both become new, for the distinction between them will have passed away.

The episode of Gog and Magog, which John introduces at this point, is a final underlining of a truth which has been present in his whole writing. The "end" is for John the outcome of man's ethical endeavor and God's apocalyptic activity. The close of the ages is His Kingdom as He brings it to pass. It is also the culmination of that Kingdom as it has come on earth. The substance of this earthly coming is in the doing of His will on earth as it is done in heaven.

Indeed, as John makes clear, this obedience rendered to God on earth is not something that is only earthly. It is of the substance of the heavenly Kingdom too. "Blessed are the dead which die in the Lord. . . . they may rest from their labours; and their works do follow them."[5]

[1] Matt. 6:10.
[2] Rev. 21:1, 5.
[3] Rom. 8:3; I Cor. 15:20; Acts 2:27-28.
[4] I Cor. 15:26; Rev. 20:10, 14.
[5] Rev. 14:13, AV.

Thy works, and alms, and all thy good endeavour,
Stayed not behind, nor in the grave were trod,
But, as Faith pointed with her golden rod,
Followed thee up to joy and bliss for ever.[6]

All obedience belongs to the Kingdom.

And, in the Kingdom? Worship shall be service, and service worship in "those great offices that suit the full-grown energies of heaven."

> "Then comes the end, when he delivers the kingdom to God the Father after destroying every rule and every authority and power."[7]

[6] John Milton, from "On the Religious Memory of Mrs. Catherine Thomson."
[7] I Cor. 15:24.

THE PROMISE OF THE NEW

"Remember not the former things,
  nor consider the things of old.
Behold, I am doing a new thing;
  now it springs forth, do you not perceive it?"[1]

A new name, a new song, a new Jerusalem, a new heaven and a new earth—that is one part of the story. The beast, the false prophet, the dragon, and finally, death and Hades, too, thrown into the lake of fire and destroyed—that is the other part of the story. God's war for righteousness, God's war against sin: the destruction of the old, the establishment of the new—this has been the theme of John and now it reaches its climax.

With one deft phrase this climax is reached and held—"and the sea was no more."[2] To the exile, on his island, the sea symbolized all his limitations. It prevented his escape, it separated him from his brethren, it was the highway across which his oppressors came. Now the sea was no more. Freedom was perfect at last, and there was nothing to fear from beyond.

The book of Revelation divides into three sections. The craftsmanship as well as the conviction of John make each section close on the same note. The first section closes with Jesus seeking entrance into human life. He stands knocking at the door.[3] The second section closes with the ark of the covenant restored to the temple.[4] Man's exile is over and God's presence with man is now secure. The third section closes with the vision of the eternal city illumined by God and by His Son.[5] All other lights and lesser lights have been put out. The presence of God is man's beatitude along the way and at the close of the journey.

Who will be there? John answers by his vision of the opening of the books. It is the only possible answer. There is judgment and God is judge. Indeed, men have no greater security than this, that their

[1] Isa. 43:18-19.
[2] Rev. 21:1.
[3] Rev. 3:20.
[4] Rev. 11:19.
[5] Rev. 21:23.

case will come to court and that wise and loving justice will be meted out to them.[6]

Our Lord's parable of the lost sheep is found in two of the Gospels.[7] In Matthew, the shepherd in the parable goes seeking his sheep "if he finds it." The possibility of the sheep being lost is acknowledged. In Luke, the shepherd goes to seek his sheep "until he finds it." No limit is set to God's redeeming power. Between these two truths men live their lives, nor may they reconcile them. Only in God are they reconciled.

> "For thou art our Father,
> though Abraham does not know us
> and Israel does not acknowledge us."[8]

[6] Luke 18:2-5.
[7] Matt. 18:10-14; Luke 15:4-7.
[8] Isa. 63:16.

THE COMING OF THE LORD

"Watch therefore, for you do not know on what day your Lord is coming."[1]

The teaching of Jesus has two sides to it: ethics and apocalypse, what God would have man do and what man can expect God to do, and these two sides of His teaching belong together. They must not be separated from each other if they are both to remain true. It is false to say that the apocalypse of the coming Kingdom is simply the result of human ethical living, just as it is false to treat human ethical living as irrelevant to the coming of the Kingdom.

"Watch," said Jesus, "because the Lord comes." "If not, I come quickly."[2]

As these white robes are soil'd and dark,
To yonder shining ground;
As this pale taper's earthly spark,
To yonder argent round;
So shows my soul before the Lamb,
My spirit before Thee,
So in mine earthly house I am,
To that I hope to be.
Break up the heavens, O Lord! and far,
Through all yon starlight keen,
Draw me, thy bride, a glittering star;
In raiment white and clean.

He lifts me to the golden doors;
The flashes come and go;
All heaven bursts her starry floors,
And strows her lights below,
And deepens on and up! the gates
Roll back, and far within
For me the Heavenly Bridegroom waits,
To make me pure of sin.

[1] Matt. 24:42.
[2] Cf. Rev. 2:16; Mark 13:18, 20.

The sabbaths of Eternity,
One sabbath deep and wide—
A light upon the shining sea—
The Bridegroom with his bride![3]

"He shall see the fruit of the travail of his soul and be satisfied."[4]

[3] Alfred Tennyson, from "St. Agnes' Eve."
[4] Isa. 53:11.

THE SEVEN BEATITUDES

"Blessed is he who reads aloud the words of the prophecy, and blessed are those who hear, and who keep what is written therein; for the time is near" (Rev. 1:3).

"Blessed are the dead who die in the Lord henceforth. Blessed indeed, says the Spirit, that they may rest from their labors, for their deeds follow them!" (Rev. 14:13.)

"Blessed is he who is awake, keeping his garments that he may not go naked and be seen exposed!" (Rev. 16:15.)

"Blessed are those who are invited to the marriage supper of the Lamb" (Rev. 19:9).

"Blessed and holy is he who shares in the first resurrection! Over such the second death has no power, but they shall be priests of God and of Christ, and they shall reign with him a thousand years" (Rev. 20:6).

"Blessed is he who keeps the words of the prophecy of this book" (Rev. 22:7).

"Blessed are those who wash their robes, that they may have the right to the tree of life and that they may enter the city by the gates" (Rev. 22:14).

BIBLIOGRAPHY

A thorough study of the book of Revelation demands the exploration of many questions. First of all there is the issue of its authorship. Whereas there is a general consensus of opinion that the Fourth Evangelist and John the seer are not the same person, this view has been challenged once again by Austin Farrer; nor can the argument of A. Edersheim be lightly set aside in which he contends that the writer of the book of Revelation must have been a priest since he shows such knowledge of the minutiae of the sacrificial worship of the temple; and that therefore it is safe to assume that he is identical with John the Apostle who probably belonged to a priestly family.

With regard to the date of the book of Revelation, once again while the present general consensus of opinion is that it was written during the last years of the reign of Domitian (A.D. 95-96), Charles C. Torrey argues for the earlier date—soon after Nero in the reign of Galba (A.D. 69) and before the destruction of Jerusalem—the date suggested by earlier scholars like H. B. Swete, B. F. Westcott, R. H. Lightfoot, and F. J. A. Hort. Torrey also argues for an original written in Aramaic which was then translated into Geek by a translator who was so faithful to the Aramaic that he even followed Aramaic syntax in his translation.

The immediate question that faces a student of the book of Revelation is whether the text as found in the Bible is in sequence. Many scholars contend that the sequence has been disturbed by an editor and seek, therefore, various transpositions of the text in order to restore that sequence. Two of the significant discussions of this subject will be found in *The Revelation of St. John (International Critical Commentary)* by R. H. Charles and in the commentary *Book of Revelation* by John Oman. On the other hand, Hanns Lilje, in his recent book, has shown that no transpositions of the text are necessary, and that the present sequence of the text is established by the simple fact that, on its basis, the structure of the book in terms of "series of seven" becomes evident.

This use of the "series of seven" as the method of understanding the structure of the book of Revelation is a feature of most commentators. In the October, 1955, issue of *Interpretation*, John Wick Bowman has a close discussion of the various ways adopted by commentators who use this method. Austin Farrer contends, however, that the pattern of the book of Revelation is not a numerical arrangement at all but a liturgical one, and proceeds to show how the daily and festal liturgies underlie the way in which the visions in the book follow one another.

A special section in the book of Revelation is the series of letters to the seven churches. The book of W. M. Ramsay on these letters, although published in 1914, will still repay study. A great deal of fresh material not found in Ramsay's book will be found in Hanns Lilje's and in Barclay's. Three additional books listed below deal with the meaning and significance of these letters, as well as discuss the "bride" and "Eucharist" themes of the book as a whole.

There are numerous general volumes on the book of Revelation which seek to take the reader through the book without burdening him with too detailed discussion about the many puzzles in it. In this category are the works by Hanns Lilje, A. S. Peake and Ernest F. Scott. Also, in this connection must be mentioned the commentary by Martin Kiddle in the Moffatt series and the commentary by R. H. Preston and A. T. Hanson in the Torch Bible series. Two books by G. W. Thorn and H. L. Goudge preach the book of Revelation to the present day.

A new translation of the book of Revelation by J. B. Phillips, with subtitles for the various units of the book, is of tremendous help to the ordinary reader. It is suggestive, also, to compare this with the way in which the book of Revelation is set out by R. G. Moulton in *The Modern Reader's Bible,* and its literary form discussed by him.

Anon. (member of Church of India). *A Door Opened in Heaven.* India: Basel Mission Press, n.d.

Barclay, William. *Letters to the Seven Churches.* London: SCM Press, 1957.

Bowman, John Wick. *The Drama of the Book of Revelation.* Philadelphia: Westminster Press, 1955.

Charles, R. H. *The Revelation of St. John* (2 vols., *International Critical Commentary*). London: T. and T. Clark, 1920.

Chavasse, Claude. *The Bride of Christ.* London: Faber and Faber, 1940.

Edersheim, A. *The Temple at the Time of Jesus.* New Jersey: Fleming H. Revell Company, 1874.

Farrer, Austin. *A Rebirth of Images.* London: Dacre Press, 1949.

Goudge, H. L. *The Apocalypse and the Present Age.* London: Mowbray, 1935.

Kiddle, Martin. *The Revelation of St. John.* New York: Harper & Brothers, 1941.

Lilje, Hanns. *The Last Book of the Bible.* Philadelphia: Muhlenberg Press, 1955.

Moulton, R. G. *Literary Study of the Bible*. Boston: D. C. Heath and Company, 1896.

Moulton, R. G. (ed.). *The Modern Reader's Bible*. London: The Macmillan Company, 1898.

Oman, John, *Book of Revelation*. Cambridge: Cambridge University Press, 1923.

Peake, A. S. *The Revelation of John*. London: Holborn Press, 1920.

Preston, R. H., and Hanson, A. T. *The Revelation of Saint John the Divine* (Torch Bible Commentaries). London: SCM Press, 1949.

Phillips, J. B. (trans.). *The Book of Revelation*. London: Geoffrey Bles, 1957.

Ramsay, W. M. *The Letters to the Seven Churches*. London: Hodder and Stoughton, 1914.

Scott, Ernest F. *The Book of Revelation*. New York: Charles Scribner's Sons, 1940.

Thorn, G. W. *Visions of Hope and Fear*. New York: George H. Doran Company, 1936.

Torrey, Charles C. *The Apocalypse of John*. New Haven: Yale University Press, 1958.

Waddy, Stacy. *The Drama of the Eucharist*. London: S.P.C.K., 1935.

SCRIPTURE INDEX

OLD TESTAMENT

Scripture Index

NEW TESTAMENT

Scripture Index

Pseudepigrapha

SUBJECT INDEX

Scripture references appearing in parentheses indicate passages in the book of Revelation.